"*The Baker Compact Di...* that—a nice, handy, qui... ary concepts, key people, ... to biblical studies. These categories of discussion often float in the underbrush of interpretation. This dictionary makes those elements accessible to those who want to know about them. This is a great supplement and starting place for giving depth to the historical and interpretive backdrop to your study of the Bible."

Darrell L. Bock, Executive Director for Cultural
Engagement, Howard G. Hendricks Center
for Christian Leadership and Cultural Engagement;
senior research professor of New Testament studies,
Dallas Theological Seminary

"*The Baker Compact Dictionary of Biblical Studies* is an ideal source for students of scripture. If one has questions about the impact of a famous scholar (such as Marcion), or the meaning of a technical term (redaction criticism), or the meaning of a strange word (Qoheleth), this dictionary provides quick and handy definitions and explanations. Here students will find clear, concise, and accurate explanations and definitions. Longman and Strauss are to be thanked for this practical resource, which will doubtless be often consulted."

Thomas R. Schreiner, James Buchanan Harrison
Professor of New Testament Interpretation,
Southern Baptist Theological Seminary

"Where does one go to find the meaning of such expressions as '*Heilsgeschichte*,' 'hendiadys,' and 'Hermetic literature'? Biblical studies literature requires a specialized dictionary. And this is precisely what Longman and Strauss have put together. This dictionary will prove to be of tremendous help to students, pastors, and teachers as they consult the rich resource materials available in biblical studies. Having ready access to this dictionary will enable you to read the literature with far greater understanding."

Clinton E. Arnold, dean and professor of New Testament, Talbot School of Theology, Biola University

"This handy work by trustworthy scholars is encyclopedic in its range of topics, yet it offers a concise, one-volume treatment valuable for students and professors alike."

Craig S. Keener, F. M. and Ada Thompson Professor of Biblical Studies, Asbury Theological Seminary

"As a student, entering the world of biblical studies, with its voluminous technical vocabulary, may seem like stepping onto the streets of a foreign country, with unintelligible signposts and incomprehensible conversations. What you need is a translator and teacher who can orient you to the language of the biblical-studies culture with short, crystal-clear explanations. Enter *The Baker Compact Dictionary of Biblical Studies* by Tremper Longman and Mark Strauss. With brief, lucid entries, they will have you speaking the language of this field in no time."

George H. Guthrie, Benjamin W. Perry Professor of Bible, Union University

"Longman and Strauss, trusted and experienced biblical scholars, have produced yet another indispensable reference tool. This compact dictionary deftly guides readers through the maze of names, terms, and concepts regularly encountered in biblical and related studies. Explanations are brief, understandable, and carefully written. Without question, every serious student of the Bible needs to add this accessible and up-to-date resource to their library."

Michael J. Williams, Johanna K. and Martin J. Wyngaarden Senior Professor in Old Testament Studies, Calvin Theological Seminary

"Every field of study has its own technical jargon that, to a novice, is daunting and unclear. Longman and Strauss, experts in Old and New Testament respectively, provide a very useful, brief, but surprisingly comprehensive introduction to the terminology, concepts, people, and places of biblical studies in readable language. The dictionary will greatly ease a newcomer's entry into this important field. I wish it had been available when I started my own studies!"

David W. Baker, professor of Old Testament and Semitic languages, Ashland Theological Seminary

"It is so helpful now to have a compact dictionary that focuses not just on 'the Bible' but also on 'biblical studies,' produced by two of the foremost scholars in the two testaments. I can see my own students keeping this book within arm's reach as they pursue their coursework. It provides a ready and reliable reference on the ancient literature to which biblical scholarship commonly refers, the major contributions for which commonly quoted names are known, the tools and terms that constitute the basic vocabulary of particular kinds of biblical criticism, sites important in Scripture or in the world of its authors, and a great deal more. This will prove a welcome aid to equip those who want to engage academic biblical literature meet the challenges of the 'learning curve' inherent in reading, for example, a critical commentary or academic article."

David A. deSilva, Trustees' Distinguished Professor of New Testament and Greek, Ashland Theological Seminary

"It was a joy to read through this dictionary as a professor. I think this reference will prove to be a rare thing: a genuinely valuable resource for new students of theology. I can imagine them thumbing through it twenty times a day as they study (and even during lectures!). I might require it for some of my classes. You should give it a look."

George Schwab, professor of Old Testament,
Erskine Theological Seminary

"Why consult a Bible dictionary in a Google-driven age? Because websites are so erratic and uneven in their quality. Longman and Strauss are trusted Old Testament and New Testament guides. From technical terms to archeology, from figures of speech to critical methods, from Bible translations to theological topics, from key scholars to eras of history, this dictionary supplies succinct, accurate, and readable summaries of the most important items a serious reader of the Bible might want to understand. Highly recommended."

Craig L. Blomberg, Distinguished Professor
of New Testament, Denver Seminary

THE BAKER
COMPACT
DICTIONARY
OF
BIBLICAL
STUDIES

Tremper Longman III
and Mark L. Strauss

BakerBooks

a division of Baker Publishing Group
Grand Rapids, Michigan

© 2018 by Tremper Longman III and Mark L. Strauss

Published by Baker Books
a division of Baker Publishing Group
PO Box 6287, Grand Rapids, MI 49516-6287
www.bakerbooks.com

Printed in the United States of America

Library of Congress Cataloging-in-Publication Data
Names: Longman, Tremper, author. | Strauss, Mark L., 1959– author.
Title: The Baker compact dictionary of biblical studies / Tremper Longman III
    and Mark L. Strauss.
Description: Grand Rapids : Baker Publishing Group, 2018.
Identifiers: LCCN 2017045541 | ISBN 9780801019074 (pbk.)
Subjects: LCSH: Bible—Criticism, interpretation, etc.—Dictionaries.
Classification: LCC BS440 .L655 2018 | DDC 220.3—dc23
LC record available at https://lccn.loc.gov/2017045541

18 19 20 21 22 23 24   7 6 5 4 3 2 1

green press INITIATIVE

Contents

Preface

Years have passed since we began our study of the Bible in an academic setting. However, we can remember the excitement of embarking on what has been and continues to be, for both of us, a rewarding and interesting career. After all, our job is basically to study the Word of God all day and to share our insights with others through our teaching and writing. We are both thankful.

Our start, though, was not so long ago that we have forgotten the barrage of new methods, scholars, terms, ideas, theories, and more that seemed so hard to remember and master from the time we were first introduced to them: form criticism, deconstruction, typology, revolution model, William Foxwell Albright, merism, colon, pericope, Zoroastrianism, and the list can go on and on. We have written this compact dictionary primarily to help beginning students. But we hope that it can help others as well, particularly pastors and laypeople who want to read and benefit from biblical scholarship.

We began our work by choosing the topics to be covered. Not an easy task. As longtime college and seminary professors of the Old (Tremper) and the New (Mark) Testaments, we asked ourselves what topics we expected our students to know about at the end of their first year of study of the Bible in an academic environment.

Once we chose the topics, we then wrote brief descriptions of them. We do not provide a detailed and extensive accounting of them but rather what we would expect our first-year students to know. This is a compact dictionary, after all, to be used as a quick-reference guide to the various topics covered here. This guide can be used as an introduction to these topics or as a review.

We hope that you find *The Baker Compact Dictionary of Biblical Studies* helpful in your study, whether you are just beginning or are further along. The Bible is God's Word and deserves to be not only read but deeply explored.

Tremper Longman III
Robert H. Gundry Professor of Biblical Studies
Westmont College

Mark L. Strauss
University Professor of New Testament
Bethel Seminary, San Diego

Abbreviations

General

//	parallel	Heb.	Hebrew
§	section	i.e.	*id est*, that is
adj.	adjective	ms(s).	manuscript(s)
ca.	circa	n.	noun
cf.	*confer*, compare	par.	and parallel(s)
chap(s).	chapter(s)	pl.	plural
e.g.	*exempli gratia*, for example	sg.	singular
		v(v).	verse(s)
Gk.	Greek		

Biblical Texts and Versions

ASV	American Standard Version	CSB	Christian Standard Bible
AV	Authorized Version	ESV	English Standard Version
CEB	Common English Bible	GNT	Good News Translation
CEV	Contemporary English Version	JPS	Jewish Publication Society Version

KJV	King James Version	NRSV	New Revised Standard Version
LXX	Septuagint		
NASB	New American Standard Bible	NT	New Testament
		OT	Old Testament
NIV	New International Version	RSV	Revised Standard Version
NJPS	New Jewish Publication Society Version	RV	Revised Version
		TEV	Today's English Version
NKJV	New King James Version	TNIV	Today's New International Version
NLT	New Living Translation		

Old Testament

Gen.	Genesis	Job	Job
Exod.	Exodus	Ps(s).	Psalm(s)
Lev.	Leviticus	Prov.	Proverbs
Num.	Numbers	Eccles.	Ecclesiastes
Deut.	Deuteronomy	Song	Song of Songs
Josh.	Joshua	Isa.	Isaiah
Judg.	Judges	Jer.	Jeremiah
Ruth	Ruth	Lam.	Lamentations
1 Sam.	1 Samuel	Ezek.	Ezekiel
2 Sam.	2 Samuel	Dan.	Daniel
1 Kings	1 Kings	Hosea	Hosea
2 Kings	2 Kings	Joel	Joel
1 Chron.	1 Chronicles	Amos	Amos
2 Chron.	2 Chronicles	Obad.	Obadiah
Ezra	Ezra	Jon.	Jonah
Neh.	Nehemiah	Mic.	Micah
Esther	Esther	Nah.	Nahum

Hab.	Habakkuk	Zech.	Zechariah
Zeph.	Zephaniah	Mal.	Malachi
Hag.	Haggai		

New Testament

Matt.	Matthew	1 Tim.	1 Timothy
Mark	Mark	2 Tim.	2 Timothy
Luke	Luke	Titus	Titus
John	John	Philem.	Philemon
Acts	Acts	Heb.	Hebrews
Rom.	Romans	James	James
1 Cor.	1 Corinthians	1 Pet.	1 Peter
2 Cor.	2 Corinthians	2 Pet.	2 Peter
Gal.	Galatians	1 John	1 John
Eph.	Ephesians	2 John	2 John
Phil.	Philippians	3 John	3 John
Col.	Colossians	Jude	Jude
1 Thess.	1 Thessalonians	Rev.	Revelation
2 Thess.	2 Thessalonians		

Apocrypha and Septuagint

Sir.	Sirach	1 Macc.	1 Maccabees

Old Testament Pseudepigrapha

Pss. Sol.	*Psalms of Solomon*

Mishnah and Talmud

b.	Babylonian Talmud	*'Abot*	*'Abot*
m.	Mishnah	*Shabb.*	*Shabbat*

Secondary Sources

COS *The Context of Scripture*. Edited by William W. Hallo. 3 vols. Leiden: Brill, 1997–2002.

A

A *See* Codex Alexandrinus (A).

א *See* Codex Sinaiticus (א).

abomination of desolation The phrase "abomination of desolation" or "devastating sacrilege" comes from the book of Daniel (9:27; 11:31; 12:11; cf. 1 Macc. 1:54), where it originally referred to the actions of the Syrian ruler Antiochus IV "Epiphanes" in desecrating the temple of Jerusalem in 167 BC, provoking the Maccabean revolt (cf. 1 Macc. 1:41–64). Antiochus's actions likely involved the placing of idols in the temple compound and the sacrifice of unclean animals on the altar of the temple. Jesus subsequently used the phrase in his Olivet Discourse in Mark 13:14 (// Matt. 24:15). It is debated as to what Jesus is referring to. Some identify it with an event in the early first century, such as Pilate's actions in bringing Roman standards into Jerusalem (ca. AD 26) or Caligula's decision to place a statue of himself in the Jerusalem Temple (ca. AD 39–40). Many others claim it refers to some event related to the siege and destruction of Jerusalem in AD 70, either committed by the Jewish rebels themselves or by the Romans. Still others place the event in the eschatological future and apply it to a still-future antichrist. *See also* Maccabees, Maccabean revolt.

acrostic In the Hebrew Bible, an acrostic is a poem in which the first unit (it could be a colon or a line) begins with the first letter of the alphabet and each successive unit begins with the next

1

letter in the alphabet (also called an abecedary). The creation of an acrostic takes great poetic skill and may be a way to indicate extensive coverage of a topic (*a* to *z*), aid memorization, or show order. Psalm 119 may be the best-known acrostic in the Hebrew Bible, composed of twenty-two stanzas (one for each letter of the Hebrew alphabet) of eight verses each, and each of the eight verses starts with the same letter before the poet moves on to the next stanza, the verses of which all begin with the next letter. (Other acrostic psalms include 9 and 10 [which together compose a single acrostic, suggesting that they were originally one psalm], 25, 34, 37, 111, 112, 119, and 145.) The final verses of Proverbs, known as the "song concerning the virtuous woman" (Prov. 31:10–31), are an acrostic poem. The first four chapters of Lamentations are each in an acrostic form. The twenty-two verses of chapters 1, 2, and 4 each start with a successive letter of the Hebrew alphabet. Chapter 3 has sixty-six verses, each successive letter beginning three consecutive verses. Chapter 5 also has twenty-two verses but is not an acrostic, perhaps indicating that there is no reconciliation between God and Israel at the end. Nahum 1 also has a broken acrostic as it describes God the warrior who melts mountains, dries up rivers, and also breaks up acrostics! *See also* colon, cola; poetry.

AD *See* BCE/CE, BC/AD.

Adapa The lead character in a Mesopotamian story known by his name (Adapa Legend). In the story, Adapa, while out in a boat, breaks the wing of the south wind to save his life. As a result he is taken to heaven and offered food by Anu, the god of heaven. If he ate the food Anu offered, he would have eternal life, but he refuses on the advice of his personal god, Ea, the god of wisdom. We do not know what motivated Ea to prevent the man Adapa from eating the food to gain eternal life except to keep him as a devotee rather than let him become a divine peer. Encouraged by the similarity of his name to Adam, some have compared the story to Genesis 3, where Adam loses the opportunity for eternal life by eating the forbidden fruit of the tree of the knowledge of good and evil. Other scholars consider the similarities to be superficial.

agrapha A Greek term (sg.: agraphon) meaning "unwritten" and referring to sayings of Jesus that do not appear in the canonical Gospels but are cited elsewhere in the NT or in other writings. For example, in Acts 20:35 Paul reminds his hearers of "the words of the Lord Jesus, because he said, 'It is more blessed to give than to receive.'" This saying of Jesus does not appear in the Gospels.

Ahasuerus (Xerxes) Ahasuerus is the Hebrew name of a Persian king (486–465 BC), also known in Greek as Xerxes, who plays an important role in the book of Esther. The book begins by recounting a huge banquet Ahasuerus gives for the leaders of his kingdom, a banquet that may be the same as one described by the Greek historian Herodotus, who mentions a large banquet before a military campaign against the Greeks. Ahasuerus's queen, Vashti, refuses to make an appearance, and so he deposes her. He replaces her with Esther. Ahasuerus's high official Haman persuades the king to issue a decree to kill all the Jews in his kingdom. They choose a date based on the casting of the *purim*, a term for lots. In the meantime, Esther reveals the deeper plot of Haman (and, perhaps for the first time, that she herself is Jewish), and so the king executes Haman, allows the Jews to defeat their enemies, and also promotes Mordecai, Esther's cousin, to a high position.

Ai First mentioned as a location near where Abraham lived for a time (Gen. 12:8; 13:3), Ai plays an important role in the conquest narrative (particularly Josh. 7–8). After defeating Jericho, Joshua sent a contingent of troops against Ai, but they were soundly defeated. God informed Joshua that they lost because someone stole some of the plunder from Jericho in violation of the laws of warfare (Deut. 7:17–26). After the culprit, a man named Achan, was discovered and executed, the Israelites successfully defeated Ai. The name Ai means "ruin" and indicates the city was not very powerful, thus illustrating that when Israel disobeys God, it cannot defeat even the weakest city. While Ai is typically associated with et-Tell, archaeologists have not been able to find remains from the time period associated with the conquest. While this lack of evidence leads some scholars to doubt the historical accuracy of Joshua 7–8, others suggest that perhaps the correlation between et-Tell and Ai is faulty.

Akitu Festival There is some evidence for an annual New Year's ritual in Babylon known as the Akitu Festival. The basic principle of the festival was the temporary undermining of order into chaos in order to reestablish that order. For instance, through priestly actions, the chief god Marduk's temple (Esagila) was ritually destroyed and then ritually built again. The king was divested of his royal power (by having his scepter and crown taken), humiliated (slapped in the face), and then returned to power (by having his regalia returned to him). Some believe that this also corresponds to Marduk's being proclaimed king of the pantheon once again. Sigmund Mowinckel believed that the biblical book of Psalms was the libretto to an Israelite version of the Akitu Festival that included an annual reenthronement of Yahweh as God. Today most people reject Mowinckel's conclusions as too speculative, but they are still widely discussed. *See also* Mowinckel, Sigmund.

Akkadian We first know Akkadian as the language of a Semitic people who lived in southern Mesopotamia in the second half of the third millennium BC and who enjoyed temporary leadership over the native Sumerian population from about 2350 to 2150. The Akkadians adopted the cuneiform writing system of the Sumerians but used the symbols to represent syllables rather than words. The Babylonian and Assyrian Empires, which ebbed and flowed from the early part of the second millennium BC until 539 BC, spoke and wrote Akkadian. Akkadian was the lingua franca of the ancient Near East from around the eighteenth century BC until it was replaced by Aramaic in the late seventh century BC. That said, Akkadian continued as a written language, particularly among those who were experts in divinatory practices like astrology, until AD 90. *See also* Aram, Aramaic; Assyria; Babylon; Sumer.

Albright, William Foxwell (1891–1971) The most influential American OT scholar and archaeologist of the first half of the twentieth century. Over against German scholarship skeptical of biblical history, he defended its "essential historicity." Albright utilized the archaeological results of his day, including ancient Near Eastern parallels (particularly from Mari and Nuzi), to bolster the claim of the basic reliability of the history of the OT, particularly the earlier periods. Albright's importance extends to the fact that he trained many of the next generation of OT scholars. *See also* Mari; Nuzi.

Alexandrian school Approach to the interpretation of the Bible that developed in Alexandria, Egypt, an early Christian center of study and education. It is especially associated with the third-century church fathers Clement of Alexandria and Origen and is known especially for its allegorical interpretation, seeking deeper spiritual truths in Scripture. The Alexandrian school is often contrasted with the Antiochene (or Antiochian) school in Antioch, Syria, which focused more on a single meaning or literal interpretation of Scripture. Key representatives of the Antiochian school include John Chrysostom and Theodore of Mopsuestia. The differences between the two schools have perhaps been overblown among modern interpreters, who tend to impose contemporary hermeneutical categories on ancient writers. *See also* allegory; Clement of Alexandria; Origen.

Alexandrian text type The family of Greek NT manuscripts considered by most NT scholars to be closest to the original autographs. Two main factors favor the Alexandrian text. First is the external evidence: Alexandrian readings tend to appear in our earliest manuscripts, including some very early papyrus manuscripts. Second is the internal evidence: Alexandrian readings tend to show the least evidence of scribal alteration. *See also* autograph; Byzantine text type; Codex Sinaiticus (ℵ); Codex Vaticanus (B); critical text; textual criticism.

allegory A story that can be interpreted to reveal a hidden or symbolic meaning. People or things in an allegory often point spiritually or symbolically to people or things in the real world. A famous OT allegory is Nathan's parable told to King David of a rich man who stole and killed a poor man's lamb (2 Sam. 12:1–4). The parable symbolically represents David arranging the murder of Uriah the Hittite and taking his wife, Bathsheba, as his own. In the NT, Jesus's parable of the tenant farmers in Mark 12:1–12 (par.) allegorically depicts the rejection of Jesus by the religious leaders of Israel. The vineyard represents the nation Israel; the owner of the vineyard is God; the tenant farmers are the religious leaders; the servants are the prophets; and the rejected son is Jesus. This parable, in turn, is based on Isaiah's allegorical Song of the Vineyard in Isaiah 5:1–6. Other biblical allegories are found in Ezekiel 17:1–24; Daniel 2:31–45; 7:1–28; 8:1–27; Galatians 4:21–31; and in many of Jesus's parables.

While these are legitimate allegories, throughout history there has been much exegetical abuse in identifying allegorical features in the biblical text that were never intended by their authors. The Alexandrian school of Alexandria, Egypt, in the third century had strong allegorizing tendencies. German NT scholar Adolf Jülicher (1857–1938) rejected allegorical interpretations of Jesus's parables and claimed that any allegorical features were accretions by the later church. This, however, would seem to be an overreaction to the problem of extreme allegorization. There is no reason to assume ahead of time that Jesus would not have used allegorization in the same way the prophets before him did. *See also* Alexandrian school; parable.

alliteration A poetic device in which the poet uses repeated consonants or related consonants to produce similar sounds in a poetic line, bringing cohesion to that line. An example may be seen in the repeated "s" and "sh" sounds in Nahum 1:10 (*Ki 'ad-dirim debukim* *ukesabe'am sarim 'ukelu keqash yabesh male*; "They will be consumed like entangled thorns, like the drink of a drunkard and like straw that is full dry"). Perhaps the repeated "s" and "sh" sounds of this verse also intend to mimic the slurry speech of a drunk person. *See also* poetry.

allusion A literary device in which a later text echoes an earlier one. An allusion is not a quotation that cites an earlier text. In an allusion there are familiar and recognizable elements of the earlier text, but also dissimilarities. For an allusion to work, the author and the audience have to share knowledge of the earlier text. In Romans 8:20 Paul speaks of "the creation" that "was subjected to futility" (*mataiotēs*). Here we see an allusion to Genesis 3 and the account of the fall, as well as to the book of Ecclesiastes, which in its Greek version pronounces that "everything is meaningless" (*mataiotēs*; 1:2). *See also* intertextuality.

Alt, Albrecht (1883–1956) After stints at other universities, Alt spent most of his career as professor of the OT at the University of Leipzig. Among his numerous contributions, Alt, along with his student Martin Noth, developed what today is called the immigration theory of Israel's emergence in Palestine. He was struck by a lack of archaeological evidence for a violent takeover, so he argued that what came to be known as Israel were people who peacefully immigrated into Palestine and eventually took over. Few, if any, hold this model of the emergence of Israel today, but it was the first of the alternative models to the conquest presented by the book of Joshua. *See also* Noth, Martin.

altar As the Hebrew term implies (*mizbeah*, from the Heb. verb *zabah*, "to sacrifice"), an altar is a place of sacrifice. The first mention of an altar in the OT comes when Noah leaves the ark and makes a sacrifice to God (Gen. 8:20), though an altar is implied in the Cain and Abel narrative (4:1–16), since they both bring sacrifices to God. Simple altars of dirt or undressed stone (Exod. 20:24–26) were built by God's people from the earliest times. The tabernacle had an altar of incense in the tent (30:1–10) and a bronze altar for animal sacrifices outside (27:1–8). The so-called law of centralization (Deut. 12) looked forward to the day when God would establish Israel firmly in the land ("rest from all the enemies around you," 12:10), and rather than multiple altars there would only be one where sacrifices could be legitimately offered. God used David to bring rest from Israel's enemies and allowed Solomon to build the temple, a permanent house, where the one altar would be found. Unfortunately, as the book of Kings pointed out, Israel often violated the law of centralization, and this was one of the reasons why God allowed the Assyrians to conquer the northern kingdom and the Babylonians to conquer the southern kingdom. At the time of the Babylonian defeat of Jerusalem, the temple was destroyed, but it was rebuilt in the immediate postexilic period, the altar being among the first things to be constructed (Ezra 3:1–6). The temple at the time of Jesus had an altar on which sacrifices were offered, but this temple was destroyed by the Romans in AD 70.

Alter, Robert (1935–) Formerly a professor of comparative literature at the University of California, Berkeley, and before that Columbia University. While Alter wrote extensively on modern Western literature, he is best known in biblical studies for his literary analyses of both Hebrew prose and poetry. Indeed, he was a very early advocate of the modern literary approach to biblical interpretation, which treated biblical texts as (composite) wholes rather than seeking to dissect the text into sources (see especially *The Art of Biblical Narrative* [Basic Books, 1981]; *The Art of Biblical Poetry* [Basic Books, 1985]). His studies attend to ancient Hebrew literary conventions to explicate the meaning of the biblical text. He is also well known for his translations of and commentary on various biblical books. *See also* narrative criticism.

amanuensis A professional scribe or literary assistant who would write down a document as it was being dictated by the author. Most literary works and letters in the ancient world would be written by these professional scribes. Poor people were often illiterate and so needed such scribes. Wealthy individuals would have a servant or personal secretary who served as their amanuensis. The author would often sign or leave a brief greeting at the end of a letter. In several of Paul's Letters, the apostle speaks of writing the final greeting in his own hand (cf. 1 Cor. 16:21; Gal. 6:11; Col. 4:18; 2 Thess. 3:17; Philem. 19). In Romans 16:22, Paul's amanuensis identifies himself and sends his greetings at the end of the letter: "I Tertius, who wrote this letter, greet you in the Lord." *See also* scribe, scribal.

Amarna tablets Over 380 diplomatic letters written by the kings of Canaanite city-states to Egyptian pharaohs during the fourteenth century BC. They are written in Akkadian, which was the lingua franca of the day, and they are called Amarna tablets because they were discovered in the archaeological digs at el-Amarna, ancient Akhenaten, in 1888–89. These letters were written by the political leaders of cities like Jebus (Jerusalem), Lachish, Gezer, and Shechem, who were in treaty relationship with Egypt at the time. The letters refer to, among other things, internal squabbles, but also external threats, the most intriguing being that presented by the *habiru/hapiru*. When the letters were first discovered, it was thought that *habiru* referred to the Hebrews, especially considering that these letters come near the time of the conquest (depending on when the exodus and conquest are dated). As time went on, though, it became clear that *habiru* was not an ethnic designation (like Hebrew) but rather a social category, referring to landless marauders who were a threat to civilization. Of course, the Canaanites would have thought of Joshua and the Israelite people as *habiru*, though we cannot take it as a direct reference to the Hebrews. *See also* Akkadian; conquest, the; Egypt.

amillennialism Theological perspective that sees the thousand-year reign of Christ mentioned in Revelation 20:1–7 as a symbolic period signifying Christ's spiritual reign in the church and in people's hearts throughout the whole period from the resurrection of Jesus to his second coming. *See also* dispensationalism; postmillennialism; premillennialism.

Ammon A nation-state that bordered Israel to the east of the Jordan River and north of the Dead Sea. Moab was on its southern border, and the land of Gilead, which often was a point of contention with the northern tribes of Israel, was to the north. The capital of Ammon was Rabbah. Moses avoided contact with the Ammonites as he led the Israelites from Egypt to the plains of Moab (Num. 21:24–35). At the time of the judges, the Ammonites were allied to Eglon the king of Moab, who captured the region around Jericho, but the Ammonites and Moabites were pushed out after the judge Ehud assassinated Eglon. Later in the period of the judges, God used Jephthah to push Ammonites out of Gilead (Judg. 11–12). During Saul's reign, the Ammonites took Jabesh-Gilead, but Saul successfully pushed them out (1 Sam. 11:1–11), and later David stayed home and committed adultery with Bathsheba while Joab besieged Rabbah (2 Sam. 11–12). Later Jehoshaphat king of Judah had to fight a coalition that included Ammon (2 Chron. 20). Nehemiah 4 mentions a man named Tobiah, one of Nehemiah's rivals who is identified as an Ammonite, along with the Ammonite people.

Amoraim *See* Tannaim.

anthropomorphism, anthropopathism In biblical interpretation, "anthropomorphism" refers to the ascription of human characteristics and qualities to God. In Genesis 2, for instance, God is said to breathe on dust to form the first man (v. 7), as if God had lungs, and in the account of the fall, the narrator pictures God as having limited knowledge (3:9). Elsewhere God is said to have eyes, ears, arms, and legs. These are typically understood to be anthropomorphisms, a type of metaphor rather than literal statements. On the other hand, an anthropopathism refers to the attribution of human emotions to God. Throughout Scripture, God loves, hates, grows angry, rejoices, and more. While some theologians believe that God does not really have emotions (apatheism), others believe that these indeed are emotions felt and expressed by God.

antinomian A generally pejorative term meaning "lawless" or "contrary to [*anti-*] law [*nomos*]" and referring to those who believe that Christians are not bound by moral or ethical law. It is often presented as the opposite extreme of legalism. Paul appears to be opposing antinomian tendencies at various points in his letters. In Romans 6:1–18 he condemns those who would suggest that salvation by grace provides a license to sin. Similarly, while Galatians is written to oppose Jewish exclusivity and/or legalism, Paul warns against the opposite extreme: "For you were called to be free, brothers and sisters; only don't use this freedom as an opportunity for the flesh, but serve one another through love" (Gal. 5:13). The letter of James, with its emphasis on faith that works, appears to be directed in part against those who were taking the Pauline doctrine of salvation by faith in an antinomian direction.

antithesis Something set in contrast to something else. In biblical studies, the term is especially used of Jesus's six statements in the Sermon on the Mount (Matt. 5:21–48) that contrast teaching related to the OT law with Jesus's own teaching, reflecting his clarification, expansion, or reinterpretation. The formula "You have heard that it was said . . ." is contrasted with Jesus's own teaching, "But I tell you . . ." The antitheses are closely related to Jesus's claim to be the fulfillment of the law (5:17).

antithetic parallelism *See* parallelism.

aphorism A short, pithy saying that communicates a general or proverbial truth. Some examples include "Do not judge, so that you won't be judged" (Matt. 7:1) and "No one who puts his hand to the plow and looks back is fit for the kingdom of God" (Luke 9:62). The book of Proverbs, the teaching of Jesus, and the letter of James all contain many aphorisms. The term can be used synonymously with "proverb" but often carries the added sense of something shown to be true by long usage. *See also* proverb.

Antiochene school *See* Alexandrian school.

Apocalypse, the Another name for the NT book of Revelation, from the Greek word for "revelation" (*apokalypsis*). The book begins, "The revelation [*apokalypsis*] of Jesus Christ that God gave him to show his servants . . ." (Rev. 1:1). *See also* apocalypticism, apocalyptic literature.

apocalypticism, apocalyptic literature Apocalypticism (from the Gk. *apokalypsis*, meaning "unveiling" or "revelation") was a Jewish movement that arose especially during the Second Temple period and emphasized God's imminent intervention in human history to judge the wicked, reward the righteous, and establish God's kingdom on earth. The term "apocalyptic" comes from the book of Revelation, which in Greek is known as the *Apocalypsis*. It was then applied anachronistically to the earlier literary genre. Apocalyptic literature was generally written in times of national crisis, when God's people were under severe threat of persecution and even eradication (especially during the persecutions of the Seleucid ruler Antiochus IV "Epiphanes"). Jewish apocalyptic works are usually pseudonymous, attributed to great OT worthies like Noah's ancestor Enoch, the prophet Ezra, and Jeremiah's scribe Baruch. Precedent for apocalyptic literature comes from eschatological passages in the OT, especially those found in Isaiah, Ezekiel, Daniel, and Zechariah. Like the book of Revelation, apocalyptic literature often features angelic hierarchies and heavenly figures as God's agents of revelation. Symbolic and mythological features are common.

Apocrypha, the The term "apocrypha" comes from a Greek word that means "hidden," perhaps referring to the fact that some believed that these books were obscure in their origin. The most typical use of the term refers to intertestamental books that are considered authoritative (deuterocanonical in the sense of being a second set of canonical books after the OT and before the NT) by the Roman Catholic Church. The list of books includes Tobit, Judith, the Greek version of Esther, Wisdom of Solomon, Sirach, Baruch, Letter of Jeremiah, Prayer of Azariah and Hymn of the Three Young Men, Susanna, and Bel and the Dragon, as well as 1 and 2 Maccabees. While these books appear in early manuscripts of the Septuagint around AD 400, they were never accepted as authoritative by the Jewish community. For this reason, Protestants believe that they are not canonical, though they are edifying. *See also* Pseudepigrapha, the.

apodictic law Apodictic law, as opposed to casuistic law, was in the form of universally valid ethical principles. Israelite law was distinct from ancient Near Eastern law collections (like the Code of Hammurabi) in having apodictic law, the most notable being the Ten Commandments (e.g., "Do not murder," Exod. 20:13). *See also* casuistic law.

apodosis *See* conditional sentence.

apostolic fathers The generation of Christian writers and theologians that came after the generation of the apostles. The collection of books that goes by the name Apostolic Fathers usually includes the following works: *1 and 2 Clement*, the letters of Ignatius of Antioch, *The Letter of Polycarp to the Philippians*, *The Martyrdom of Polycarp*, *The Didache*, *The Epistle of Barnabas*, *The Shepherd of Hermas*, *The Epistle to Diognetus*, the fragment of Quadratus of Athens, and the fragments of Papias of Hierapolis.

apparatus, critical In biblical studies, a critical apparatus is a set of notes accompanying Greek or Hebrew texts that includes textual variants and supporting documentation. The most widely used Hebrew Bible with a critical apparatus is the *Biblia Hebraica Stuttgartensia* (4th edition). The standard critical Greek New Testaments are the United Bible Societies (5th edition) and the Nestle-Aland (28th edition) texts. See also *Biblia Hebraica Stuttgartensia (BHS)*; critical text.

Apsu In the Enuma Elish, Apsu and his consort Tiamat are primordial deities, who are there at the beginning. Apsu and Tiamat represent the primordial waters. They give birth to the next generation of gods and goddesses, but then Apsu determines to do away with his divine children because they make too much noise. Tiamat tries to dissuade him, but before he can act, the god Ea discovers the plot and kills him, building his throne upon Apsu (see the similar image of Yahweh's throne established on the flood waters in Ps. 29:10). *See also* Enuma Elish; Tiamat.

Aquila of Sinope A translator of the Hebrew Bible into Greek. His translation, produced around AD 130, was included in Origen's *Hexapla* (six translations side by side). Only fragments of Aquila's work survive today. While the Greek translation of Symmachus was more idiomatic Greek, Aquila's was more literal. Christians did not generally like it, claiming it downplayed the messianic prophecies. Yet Origen valued it enough to include it in his work. Epiphanius claimed Aquila was a Jewish proselyte, a relative of the Roman emperor Hadrian who first converted to Christianity and then to Judaism. He became a disciple of the famous Rabbi Akiba. See also *Hexapla*; Origen; Septuagint; Symmachus; Theodotion.

Arabic A Semitic language, related to Hebrew. The earliest Arabic comes from pre-Islamic times (before the seventh century AD), but we have virtually nothing that comes from the OT period. Even so, Arabic is a conservative language preserving many of the characteristics of the hypothetical earliest Semitic (like having thirty letters/phonemes). Thus, the main contribution that the study of Arabic makes to OT studies is to provide cognates to Hebrew that help deepen our understanding of the meaning of ancient Hebrew words.

Arad ostraca Since the early 1960s archaeologists have discovered over one hundred ostraca written in Hebrew at the site of ancient Arad, a city in the Negev about seventeen miles northeast of Beersheba. A number of them are inscriptions that functioned as communication between military personnel and date to the crisis period just before the Babylonian military intervention to put down a revolt initiated by King Jehoiakim (598 BC). There is mention of a threat from Edom to the east. *See also* ostraca.

Aram, Aramaic Aram refers to tribal elements and small nation-states that appeared in (what was later known as) Syria beginning around the thirteenth century BC, though they probably came from Upper Mesopotamia, the native homeland of Abraham's family (see reference to him as a "wandering Aramean," Deut. 26:5). Among its most important cities was Damascus. The Arameans threatened Israel during the time of Saul and David (1 Sam. 14:47 [Zobah]; 2 Sam. 8:3–8, 10–12) and were often in conflict with the northern kingdom of Israel, particularly during the early periods of the divided monarchy (1 Kings 22:1–38).

Their language, Aramaic, is very similar to Hebrew, both being Northwest Semitic languages. Since the Chaldean tribe that assumed dominance in Lower Mesopotamia (Babylon) in the seventh century BC spoke Aramaic as their native tongue, Aramaic replaced Akkadian as the lingua franca as Babylon under Nabopolassar and then his son Nebuchadnezzar assumed dominance in the Near East. Ezra 4:8–6:18; 7:12–26; and Daniel 2:4–7:28 as well as a few isolated verses of the OT are in Aramaic. By Jesus's day, Aramaic had replaced Hebrew as the common language of the Jewish people, and there are a number of words and phrases transliterated from Aramaic in the NT (e.g., Mark 5:41; 7:34; 14:35; Rom. 8:15). *See also* Akkadian; Hebrew language; Northwest Semitic.

archaeology The discovery, recovery, and analysis of material remains from the past. The modern discipline of archaeology relevant for the study of the Bible began in the early nineteenth century, though at first it was little more than scavenging. Archaeological work over the past two centuries has helped us recover literary and cultural artifacts that have given us a better understanding of Israel and its surrounding cultures and have proved illuminating for the study of the OT and NT. The interpretation of archaeological materials is often controversial, and attempts to marshal archaeology to prove or disprove the Bible are a misuse and not determinative. Archaeology uses some scientific methods (e.g., carbon dating) but is more like a social science or even a subdiscipline of history than a hard science.

aretalogy From Greek *aretē*, "virtue"; story or legend describing the miraculous or marvelous deeds of a god, a "divine man," or a human hero. The miracle stories of Jesus are sometimes compared to Greco-Roman aretalogies. *See also* divine man (*theios anēr*).

Aristeas, Letter of *See* Septuagint.

Arius, Arianism Arius (ca. 256–336) was an early Christian theologian and church leader from Alexandria, Egypt, whose controversial teachings about the nature of Jesus were the primary topic of debate at the Council of Nicaea, called by Emperor Constantine in 325. Arius claimed that God the Father was the only infinite and eternal being and that the Son had a beginning, being the first and greatest of God's creations. Through the Son (the Logos), the Father created the universe. Arius's beliefs were condemned at Nicaea.

ark of the covenant A wooden container completely covered with gold that was placed in the most holy place of the sanctuary (Exod. 25:10–22). It was forty-five inches long, twenty-seven inches wide, and twenty-seven inches high. It had golden rings through which poles were placed in order that the box might be carried by priests. The ark had cherubim figures placed on its cover. They were depicted as having outstretched wings, and their eyes were facing down, presumably because God in all his glory was thought to be enthroned above the ark, which is thought to be a kind of footstool (1 Chron. 28:2). As the piece of sanctuary furniture closest to the manifest presence of God, the ark was considered very sacred. The ark was a mobile symbol of God's presence and so was taken on the battlefield to represent the fact that God was present with the army. While the ark plays an important role in the early history of God's people, it appears that it was lost sometime before the exile, and Jeremiah announces that it will not be rebuilt (3:16).

Ashdod One of the five main Philistine cities (Josh. 13:3); the others were Gaza, Gath, Ashkelon, and Ekron. The Philistines competed with the Israelites for the Shephelah (the rolling hills between the coastal plain and the Judean mountains in southwest Israel) and the Mediterranean coast from directly west of Jerusalem down to the Sinai Peninsula. Ashdod was situated in the northern region of Philistine territory. The Philistines were particularly active from the time of Judges (especially in the story of Samson; Judg. 13–16), to the time when Eli was judge (during which time they captured the ark and took it to Ashdod; 1 Sam. 5:1–2), and down to the time of David, who fought Goliath, their champion (1 Sam. 17), and as king ultimately subdued them. The Assyrians later incorporated them into the Assyrian Empire as the province Ashdod. The prophets envisioned the destruction of Philistine cities (Jer. 25:17–20; 47:1–7; Amos 1:8; etc.). *See also* Ashkelon; Ekron; Gath; Gaza; Philistia.

Asherah   A prominent goddess worshiped by the Canaanites, as well as some apostate Israelites. Asherah, along with Anat, plays an important role in the Ugaritic texts, where she is sometimes depicted as El's consort. She appears to be a goddess of love and war. In the Bible, her worship is associated with the veneration of a pole that seems to be some type of cult object (for the Asherah pole, see Exod. 34:13; Deut. 12:3; 1 Kings 14:15; etc.). Although the Asherah poles were placed at shrines, we don't know exactly what they looked like. The prophets condemn the worship of Asherah and call for the destruction of the poles associated with her worship (Isa. 17:8; 27:9; Jer. 17:2; Mic. 5:14). Inscriptions found at Kuntillet 'Ajrud and Khirbet el-Qom may indicate that some Israelites worshiped her as the wife of Yahweh. *See also* Khirbet el-Qom inscription; Kuntillet 'Ajrud inscriptions; Ugaritic.

Ashkelon   City located in the middle of Philistine territory between Ashdod to the north and Gaza in the south. Samson went there and killed thirty Philistines in order to take their clothes to pay off a bet (Judg. 14:19). An Amarna tablet sent by the Canaanite king of Ashkelon shows that the city was a vassal of Egypt in the mid-fourteenth century BC. *See also* Amarna tablets; Ashdod; Ekron; Gath; Gaza; Philistia.

assonance While alliteration involves repeated consonantal sounds, "assonance" refers to repeated vowel sounds in a poetic line. Jeremiah, for example, asks: *Madua' yarash malkam 'et-gad we'ammo be'arayw yasab* ("Why then has Milcom dispossessed Gad and his people settled in their cities?" 49:1). Notice the repeated "a" vowels that cause this poetic line to bind together. *See also* alliteration; poetry.

Assyria In the early second millennium BC, after the collapse of the neo-Sumerian state centered on Ur (the so-called Ur III dynasty), various power centers arose in Mesopotamia, most notably around the cities of Ashur in the north and Babylon in the south. These two cities exerted their influence over their respective regions and also vied with each other for dominance throughout Mesopotamia and beyond. The Assyrians, like the Babylonians, were Semitic peoples. Besides Ashur, located on the upper Tigris, other important cities included Nineveh (featured particularly in the book of Jonah) and Calah. Although Asshur/Assyria flourished both at the beginning and at the end of the second millennium, the most important time period, at least in regard to biblical history, is the so-called neo-Assyrian period (911–612 BC). During the reign of Tiglath-pileser III (744–727 BC), Assyria expanded to incorporate Syria into its empire and threatened the northern kingdom of Israel (2 Kings 15:29). This attack initiated an alliance between the king of the north (Pekah) and the king of Syria (Rezin). When they tried to force the king of Judah (Ahaz) into the alliance, the prophet Isaiah told him not to worry about their threats (Isa. 7), but, not heeding Isaiah's warnings, Ahaz entered into an alliance with the Assyrians (2 Kings 16:10–18). Soon thereafter, in an attack initiated by Shalmaneser V (726–722 BC) and completed by Sargon II (721–705 BC), the Assyrians defeated the northern kingdom, deported its leading citizens, and brought in foreigners, who intermarried with the native population (2 Kings 17; *see* Samaria, Samaritans). While Judah maintained its monarchy, it became an Assyrian vassal. During the reign of Hezekiah, the

Assyrian king Sennacherib (704–681 BC) failed in his attempt to take Jerusalem (701 BC), but Judah maintained its vassal status (2 Kings 18:17–19:37; Isa. 36–37). The Assyrian Empire weakened during the third quarter of the seventh century BC and was eventually defeated and absorbed by the first neo-Babylonian king, Nabopolassar. While Nabopolassar first rebelled against Assyria in 626 BC, he did not defeat Nineveh until 612 BC (as foretold by Nahum), when he had the help of the Medes. The final end for Assyria came in 605 BC, when Babylon defeated a combined Assyrian-Egyptian army at Carchemish. *See also* Babylon; Sumer.

Astruc, Jean (1632–77) French physician and student of the Bible who is considered the originator of a theory of the composition of the Pentateuch eventually known as the Documentary Hypothesis. Though soon after his time the theory distanced the composition of the Pentateuch from Moses, Astruc actually used his theory of two sources to defend Mosaic authorship. He differentiated the two sources in the Pentateuch on the basis of the two names for God, Elohim and Yahweh. Yahweh, the name revealed to Moses at the burning bush (Exod. 3), characterizes the source that Moses himself wrote, while the more generic term for God, Elohim, was used in an earlier source that Moses utilized. *See also* Documentary Hypothesis; Wellhausen, Julius.

Athanasius of Alexandria (ca. 296–373) Leading Christian theologian, church father, and bishop of Alexandria. Athanasius was the chief opponent of the teachings of Arius and Arianism, which were condemned at the Council of Nicaea in 325. Athanasius was often in conflict with the Roman emperor and during his forty-five-year episcopate suffered five different exiles at the hands of four emperors. *See also* Arius, Arianism.

Atrahasis A mythological text written in Akkadian that comes from the Old Babylonian period (first half of the second millennium BC) though based on even earlier texts. The significance of Atrahasis is that it contains both an account of the creation of humanity (from the clay and the blood of a god as well as the spit of the gods) and a flood account, thus making it suitable for comparisons with Genesis 1–11. Atrahasis is the name of the flood hero and is sometimes referred to as the Babylonian Noah. *See also* Akkadian; Enuma Elish; Gilgamesh Epic.

Augustine of Hippo (354–430) Early Christian theologian, church father, and bishop of Hippo in North Africa from 395 to 430. "Saint Augustine" is widely recognized as the greatest theologian of the early church. Though he wrote on virtually every aspect of Christian theology, he is especially known for his teaching on original sin and predestination. He was a prolific writer who produced more than a hundred works. Among the most famous are his *Confessions* and *The City of God*. The latter sought to identify the church as the spiritual city of God and to encourage Christians who were in turmoil following the sack of Rome by the Visigoths in 410. Augustine was also apparently the first Christian scholar to propose a solution to the "Synoptic problem," claiming that Matthew wrote first, that Mark abbreviated Matthew, and that Luke used both. *See also* Synoptic problem.

autograph The original manuscript of a biblical composition. An evangelical doctrine of inerrancy claims that the Bible is without error in its autographs. It must be acknowledged that we do not have access to the actual autographs of biblical texts; thus an autograph is a hypothetical construct based on the actual texts that have come down through the centuries to us today. The autograph is reconstructed through the process of textual criticism. *See also* inerrancy of Scripture; textual criticism.

B

B *See* Codex Vaticanus (B).

Baal The name of the god worshiped by the native inhabitants of Syria-Palestine. The name Baal means "lord." In the Baal texts, written in Ugaritic, Baal is the son of El, who assumes the kingship of the pantheon. Baal is a storm god said to ride the clouds and provide dew and rain. As a god of fertility, he was an attractive alternative or supplement to the worship of Yahweh and thus a source of idolatry and the object of scorn of the biblical prophets. *See also* Baal texts; Ugaritic.

Baal texts Starting in 1929, a number of cuneiform texts were discovered at the ancient site of Ugarit (modern Ras Shamra). Included in these texts (written in what came to be known as Ugaritic) were texts that described the exploits of the god Baal. These texts describe Baal's defeat of the sea god Yam, his ascent to the kingship of the gods, and the building of his house (temple), as well as his death at the hands of the god named Mot (Death) and his eventual revivification. These texts have proven invaluable both for filling out the picture of the worship of Baal, frequently mentioned in the OT as a major rival to Yahweh, and for providing background to many biblical texts. *See also* Baal; Ugaritic.

Babylon In the early second millennium BC, after the collapse of the neo-Sumerian state centered on Ur (the so-called Ur III dynasty), various power centers arose in Mesopotamia, most notably around the cities of Ashur in the north and Babylon in the south. These two cities exerted their influence over their respective regions and also vied with each other for dominance throughout Mesopotamia and beyond. The Babylonians, like the Assyrians, were Semitic peoples. Starting toward the end of the second millennium, Assyria and Babylon took turns subduing each other and pushing their borders in their efforts to form an empire. In terms of biblical history, the most important phase is the so-called neo-Babylonian period (626–539 BC). After throwing off the dominance of Assyria under Nabopolassar, the Babylonian army pushed their influence into southern Syria and northern Israel under Nebuchadnezzar (605–562 BC). According to the book of Daniel, Judah with its capital in Jerusalem became a vassal state of Babylon around 605 BC. Judah's king Jehoiakim chose to revolt in 598 BC, a move quickly snuffed out by Nebuchadnezzar, who took Jehoiakim's son, who was ruling by the time Nebuchadnezzar got to Jerusalem, into exile along with a number of other leading citizens including a young priest named Ezekiel. The Babylonian king then put yet another descendant of David, Zedekiah, on the throne. He too chose to rebel against Babylon in 586 BC. This time Nebuchadnezzar brought an end to the monarchy, destroyed the palace and the town, and took more of the leading citizens into exile. He appointed a Jewish governor (Gedaliah) of the new province of Yehud. Years later the Persians under their king Cyrus conquered Babylon and inherited its vast empire, including Yehud (539 BC). In the book of Revelation Babylon stands for an evil human kingdom standing over against God (Rev. 14:8; 17:5; etc.). *See also* Akkadian; Assyria; Sumer.

Babylonian exile Starting in 605 BC (Dan. 1:1–3), Judah was a vassal state of Babylon, whose king was Nebuchadnezzar. King Jehoiakim of Judah revolted against Babylon in 598, but by the time Babylon's army arrived in Jerusalem, his son Jehoiachin was on the throne. When Nebuchadnezzar pacified the city, he deported Jehoiakim and other leading citizens to Babylon and installed Zedekiah, Jehoiakim's brother, on the throne. In 586 BC, Zedekiah rebelled against Babylon. When Nebuchadnezzar put down the revolt, he removed Zedekiah from the throne and killed his sons, bringing the monarchy to an end. He also destroyed the palace, the temple, and much of the city, deporting yet more of the leading citizens to Babylon, though leaving the poor of the land, who likely constituted the bulk of the population, to live under a Persian-appointed Jewish governor named Gedaliah (Jer. 39–45). The exiles were relocated to the heart of Babylon, though given lands and the opportunity to live established lives in Babylon, an opportunity the prophet Jeremiah encouraged them to embrace (Jer. 29). When Persia defeated Babylon, they allowed Babylon's captive vassals, including the Jews, to return to their homelands if they chose to do so (539 BC). In one important sense, this brought the exile to a close, but since the Jews continued to be dominated by a powerful nation, the exile, in another sense, was thought to continue (Dan. 9:20–27).

Bar Kokhba revolt A second Jewish revolt against the Romans from AD 132 to 135, sixty years after the first revolt, which resulted in the destruction of Jerusalem and the temple (66–73). This rebellion was the result of (1) increasing political and social conflict between the Jews and Roman administration and (2) ruthless Roman suppression of various minor revolts. The immediate provocation seems to have been the emperor Hadrian's ban on circumcision and plans to build a temple to Jupiter on the Temple Mount. The revolt was led by Simon ben Kosiba (Aramaic: bar Kosiba), who was nicknamed Bar Kokhba ("son of the star"), an allusion to the messianic prophecy of Numbers 24:17, which states that a (messianic) "star" will rise out of Jacob. The famous Rabbi Akiba went so far as to declare Bar Kokhba to be the Messiah. Despite early successes by the revolutionaries, the rebellion was eventually crushed by the Roman legions in 135. The Romans subsequently turned Jerusalem into a pagan city, and Jews were forbidden from entering.

Barr, James (1924–2006) Born in Scotland, James Barr retired from Oxford as the Regius Professor of Hebrew in 1989 but thereafter worked as professor of OT at Vanderbilt University (1989–98).

His early work *The Semantics of Biblical Literature* (1961) levied a heavy critique against weak linguistic arguments like the appeal to etymology, and he also criticized an overzealous use of cognate languages to determine the meaning of words (for which see *Comparative Philology and the Text of the Old Testament* [1968]). He was also a critic of evangelical theology (see *Fundamentalism* [1977]). *See also* etymology; Kittel, Gerhard.

Barrett, Charles Kingsley (1917–2011) One of the leading British NT scholars of the twentieth century. He became professor of NT at the University of Durham in 1958 and spent most of his career there. Among his most influential works are his commentary on John (1955) and his two-volume commentary on Acts in the International Critical Commentary series (1994, 1999). Barrett was also one of the leading Pauline scholars of his day, writing monographs on Paul and commentaries on Romans, 1 and 2 Corinthians, Galatians, and the Pastoral Epistles.

Baur, Ferdinand Christian (1792–1860) German theologian, biblical scholar, and founder of the so-called Tübingen School of biblical criticism. Baur applied the dialectic philosophy of G. W. F. Hegel (thesis-antithesis-synthesis) to the history of early Christianity. Baur claimed that early Jewish Christianity (the thesis), represented by Peter, found its opposition in Gentile Christianity (the antithesis), represented by Paul. The synthesis was reached in second-century Christianity, represented especially in Luke-Acts, where Peter and Paul are presented as allies rather than opponents. Baur is sometimes called the father of modern studies in church history.

BCE/CE, BC/AD During the Middle Ages, an absolute dating system was developed by the monk Dionysius Exiguus (470–544), which began with the birth of Christ. Dates before the birth of Christ were labeled BC (from the later English "before Christ"), and those after the birth AD (for the Latin *anno Domini*, "in the year of the Lord"). There is no year 0; the date moves from 1 BC to AD 1 (the tradition is to put BC after the number and put AD before the number). As a side note, we should point out that Jesus's birth year was incorrectly calculated (Jesus was most likely born between 7 and 4 BC). In the past couple of decades, it has become common for people to substitute BCE ("before the common era") and CE ("common era") for the more religious traditional designations.

beatitude The term comes from a Latin word meaning "blessing" or "happiness" and is the technical term applied to the eight blessings that begin the Sermon on the Mount (Matt. 5:3–12). Each beatitude begins with a blessing and then adds the reason or result of that blessing, for example, "Blessed are the poor in spirit, for the kingdom of heaven is theirs" (Matt. 5:3). Focusing on the poor, the humble, and the merciful, the Beatitudes express the great reversal that is coming as a result of the in-breaking power of the kingdom of God. Luke's version of the sermon has four beatitudes, followed by four "woes," or pronouncements of judgment against the rich, powerful, and arrogant. *See also* blessing.

Benedictus Latin title given to the song of praise recited by Zechariah, Jewish priest and father of John the Baptist, in Luke 1:68–79. The word means "blessed" or "praise be" and is the first word of the Latin version of the hymn. The Benedictus is one of four hymns of Luke's infancy narrative, all of which pick up key Lukan themes. The others are Mary's Magnificat (1:46–55), the angelic Gloria in Excelsis (2:14), and Simeon's Nunc Dimittis (2:29–32). The Benedictus is given on the occasion of the circumcision and naming of John the Baptist. It praises God for his great salvation through the coming of the Messiah from David's line and celebrates John's role as the forerunner of the Messiah. *See also* Magnificat; Nunc Dimittis.

ben Sira *See* Sirach.

Biblia Hebraica Stuttgartensia (BHS) *BHS* is the edition of the Hebrew Bible that is used for translation and for commentary and other scholarly study. It is the fourth edition produced by the German Bible Society, and it began to make its appearance book by book in the late 1960s, the whole OT being completed in 1977. The Hebrew text used in the body of *BHS* is Codex Leningradensis, which includes the masorah as well as the leading textual variants (in footnotes to the text). At present, the fifth edition (*Biblia Hebraica Quinta*) is under production and will eventually replace *BHS*. *See also* Codex Leningradensis; masorah; textual criticism.

biblical theology Since the end of the eighteenth century, scholars have treated biblical theology as a discipline that explores the development of biblical categories and themes (e.g., covenant, Divine Warrior, wisdom, kingship), especially with reference to the distinct theological emphases of persons and periods. Biblical theology thus speaks of Pauline theology, Johannine theology, or the theology of the prophets. It is primarily historical, describing truth from the perspective of individual biblical authors or movements. This is in contrast to systematic theology, which is primarily philosophical, answering questions of ultimate truth. Systematic theology often uses nonbiblical categories (e.g., Trinity, incarnation) to describe the nature of Christian truth. The scope of biblical theology and that of systematic theology are overlapping, and the difference between the two is sometimes disputed by scholars. Biblical theology tends to be more historical in its method (for instance, talking about the development of the canon). One develops a biblical theology by exegesis of the biblical text, but then one's biblical theology can also inform one's exegesis in a kind of hermeneutical spiral.

biblical theology movement The biblical theology movement is not to be confused with the biblical theological method (*see also* biblical theology). The biblical theology movement is a group of loosely associated scholars who worked from the 1930s until the 1960s, who were reacting against liberal tendencies to atomize the text into component parts through source analysis and other historical-critical methods. They did not reject these methods outright but rather turned focus onto the final form of the text. They also emphasized the historical dimension of the biblical witness (a leading slogan was "the God who acts"). They were not evangelical in their understanding of Scripture; rather, they were aligned with the Barthian view that the Bible was a witness to the Word where one could encounter the divine, but the Bible was not itself the Word of God and therefore without error in all it intends to teach.

biblicism, bibliolatry The view that the Bible itself is an object of worship. An orthodox view of the Bible is that the Bible is fully human and fully divine, that God is the ultimate author who uses human authors as vehicles of his message. However, it is quite clear from the biblical books that God allowed the individual human authors to express his Word using their own distinctive styles. The charge of "biblicism" or "bibliolatry" is typically levied by scholars and others against those whom they judge to deny or minimize the human dimensions of Scripture.

bicolon *See* colon, cola.

Birkat Haminim Hebrew phrase meaning "benediction concerning heretics" and referring to Benediction 12 of the Palestinian edition of the Eighteen Benedictions (the Shemoneh Esreh), an ancient prayer of Judaism. Benediction 12 likely arose in the late first century as a curse against "Nazarenes" (= Christians), treating them as traitors to Judaism. It reads, "And for apostates let there be no hope; and may the insolent kingdom be quickly uprooted, in our days. And may the Nazarenes and the heretics perish quickly; and may they be erased from the Book of Life." The Birkat Haminim is often discussed in the context of Matthew's Gospel, which was likely written at a time of increasing hostility and the breaking of ties between Jews and Jewish Christians. Some scholars claim that the Benediction was originally directed at other "heretics" like the Sadducees, and that the reference to the Christians was added at the Council of Jamnia during the leadership of Rabbi Gamaliel II in the late first century. *See also* Jamnia; Shemoneh Esreh (Eighteen Benedictions).

Bishops' Bible *See* King James Version (KJV).

blessing At their creation, God blessed the first human beings (Gen. 1:22, 28). To bless someone is to effectively announce that one holds favor toward them and holds them in high regard. In the case of humanity, this blessing at creation indicates a harmonious relationship to God and also with each other. God also places them in Eden, a place that satisfies all their material needs. When they rebel against God, they forfeit that blessing, but God pursues them in order to seek reconciliation. In the call of Abraham, we see that God intends to bless not only Abraham and his descendants but also "all the peoples on earth" (Gen. 12:3). Later lists of the rewards for covenant obedience also provide a window on the nature of blessing in the OT (e.g., Deut. 27–28). When humans bless God, they thus express their high regard for him; thus blessing God is similar to offering praise or worshiping him.

book of the covenant The narrator of the book of Exodus uses the term "book of the covenant" to refer to the law given to Moses on Mount Sinai (see 24:7, e.g., NRSV, NIV), and modern scholars continue to use the term to differentiate this corpus from other collections of law in the Torah. Moses wrote down the law given to him (24:4), including the Ten Commandments (20:2–27) and the case law that follows it (20:22–23:19). The case (casuistic) law applies the general ethical principles of the Ten Commandments to specific cases likely to arise among God's people during the OT period. *See also* casuistic law.

Bornkamm, Günther (1905–90) German biblical scholar and professor of NT at the University of Heidelberg. Bornkamm was a student of Rudolf Bultmann and advocate of form criticism, but he departed from his mentor in affirming the legitimacy of historical-Jesus research. Together with Ernst Käsemann and others, he helped to launch the so-called new (or second) quest for the historical Jesus. His volume *Jesus von Nazareth* (1956) is considered a classic representative of the findings of the "second quest." Bornkamm was also a pioneer in the emerging field of redaction criticism and did groundbreaking redactional work on

Matthew's Gospel. *See also* Bultmann, Rudolf Karl; new (second) quest for the historical Jesus.

Bousset, Wilhelm (1865–1920) German NT scholar and key representative of the history of religions school (*Religionsgeschichtliche Schule*) at the University of Göttingen. This school of thought sought to trace many of the beliefs of early Christianity to earlier religious traditions. Bousset's most famous work was *Kyrios Christos* (1913), in which he claimed that the high Christology of the NT arose via Hellenistic-Jewish Christianity and its contact with Greco-Roman pagan religious traditions. *See also* history of religions school (*Religionsgeschichtliche Schule*).

Bronze Age Archaeologists divide the past into different ages according to the material used for tools and weapons. The Stone (Paleo-, Meso-, and Neolithic), Copper (Chalcolithic), Bronze, and Iron Ages are relevant for the study of the OT. The Bronze Age in the ancient Near East, including Israel, begins around 3300 BC and extends to 1200 BC. The Bronze Age is divided into three periods, each of which is also further divided.

The Bronze Age

Early Period	IA-B (3300–3000 BC)
	II (3000–2700 BC)
	III (2700–2200 BC)
Middle Period	I (2200–2000 BC)
	IIA (2000–1750 BC)
	IIB (1750–1550 BC)
Late Period	I (1550–1400)
	IIA (1400–1300 BC)
	IIB (1300–1200 BC)

In Israel, this period is sometimes called the Canaanite period because it is considered the time before Joshua and the Israelites invaded Canaan. The patriarchs would likely have been in the area during the Middle Bronze IIA period. Biblical scholars argue over whether the exodus and settlement happened during the Late Bronze period or the Early Iron Age. *See also* archaeology; Iron Age.

Brown, Raymond E. (1928–98) Roman Catholic priest and one of the leading NT scholars of the twentieth century. He taught for twenty-nine years at Union Theological Seminary in New York City. Among his most influential works were his two-volume commentary on John's Gospel in the Anchor Bible Commentary (1966, 1970) and his magisterial works *The Birth of the Messiah* (1977) and *The Death of the Messiah* (1994). Brown was an important advocate of the theory of a "Johannine community" standing behind the traditions of the Fourth Gospel (see his book *The Community of the Beloved Disciple* [1979]). *See also* Johannine community.

Bruce, Frederick Fyvie (1910–90) One of the leading evangelical NT scholars of the twentieth century. After stints at the University of Edinburgh and the University of Leeds, he spent twelve years teaching at the University of Sheffield before becoming Rylands Professor of Biblical Criticism and Exegesis at Manchester University in 1959. He retired from teaching in 1978. Bruce wrote over forty books, including both popular and technical volumes. His first book, *Are the New Testament Documents Reliable?*, became an evangelical standard for NT apologetics. His specialty was the apostle Paul, although he also wrote commentaries on Hebrews and Acts and important works on the canon, NT history, and the Dead Sea Scrolls.

Brueggemann, Walter (1933–) Prolific American OT theologian who writes for both scholarly and ecclesiastical audiences. His writings span the OT canon, but he particularly focuses on Genesis and Psalms as well as Wisdom literature. His *Old Testament Theology: Testimony, Dispute, Advocacy* well illustrates his tendency to find tensions within the Bible (e.g., traditions that affirm the status quo and traditions that want to challenge the status quo) and to explore them for contemporary significance. His teaching career began at Eden Theological Seminary (1961–86) and continued at Columbia Theological Seminary in Decatur, Georgia, where he was the William Marcellus McPheeters Professor of Old Testament until his retirement in 2003, when he assumed emeritus status.

Bultmann, Rudolf Karl (1884–1976) One of the most influential NT scholars of the twentieth century. Bultmann served for thirty years as professor of NT at the University of Marburg in Germany (1921–51). Bultmann claimed that the early church had little interest in the historical Jesus. Their primary interest was in the Christ of faith, who was still speaking to the church through Christian prophets. They therefore had no trouble attributing words and deeds to Jesus that had no historical basis. Because of this we can know very little about the historical Jesus—little more, really, than that he existed. The Gospels instead give us a window into the life of the early church. Bultmann was a pioneer in NT form criticism (*Formgeschichte*), a method that seeks to trace how oral traditions were created and developed in the early church. Philosophically, Bultmann was an existentialist, claiming that the true message of Jesus was a call to decision to live an authentic existence. To discern this message, he sought to "demythologize" the NT, removing those features associated with a primitive worldview. *See also* form criticism (*Formgeschichte*).

Byzantine text type The family of Greek NT texts making up the great majority of Greek manuscripts (also known as the "majority text" and the "ecclesiastical text"). Its name "Byzantine" comes from the fact that it was the text current in Constantinople from the fourth century onward. Most scholars consider the Byzantine family to have arisen as an attempt, either by Lucian of Antioch (ca. 240–312) or during the reign of Constantine (reigned ca. 306–37), to standardize the Greek NT. Byzantine readings tend to harmonize, conflate, and smooth over earlier readings. *See also* Alexandrian text type; textual criticism; Textus Receptus.

C

Caesarean text type *See* textual criticism.

caesura A parallel line (parallelism) is composed of two or more cola (sg.: colon). The momentary pause between the cola within a parallel line is referred to as a caesura. The end of the poetic line implies a longer pause.

> If only my anguish could be weighed
> > and all my misery be placed on the scales.
> > > (Job 6:2 NIV)

See also colon, cola; parallelism; poetry.

canon An English word that ultimately derived from the Hebrew word *qaneh* (through Greek and Latin). The word means "reed," and its figurative meaning is "standard." While one must be careful of meanings derived from etymology, in this case it is illustrative. When one pronounces something canonical, one is saying it is a standard. In biblical studies, "canon" refers to those books that the church has traditionally taken as the standard of faith and practice. For Protestant Christians, the canon is composed of the thirty-nine books of the OT and twenty-seven books of the NT. Catholics and Orthodox Christians have a broader canon (*see* Apocrypha, the; Pseudepigrapha, the). The strongest argument in favor of the narrower, Protestant canon of the OT is that we inherit these Scriptures from the Jewish community, particularly rabbinical Judaism, and Jews never accepted the extra books as authoritative.

canonical criticism/approach Canonical criticism developed during the 1970s particularly under the influence of Brevard Childs, professor of OT at Yale University. Childs argued that, while historical-critical methods like source-, form-, and redaction-criticism were valuable to get at the history of the composition of the biblical text, they did not help toward understanding the meaning of the final form of the text, and that, according to Childs and his followers, was of most significance to the church. Indeed, Childs, who taught at a seminary, argued that students who went on to become clergy, while able to analyze the sources of a biblical book, found it hard to preach the theological message of the book. Canonical criticism goes even further when it encourages that any biblical book or part of a biblical book should be interpreted in the light of the entire canon. Canonical criticism, with its focus on the final form, shares many of the concerns of a literary approach to the biblical text. Historical critics express suspicion that the canonical approach simply masks a return to a precritical approach to the text, which they regard as a type of fundamentalism. Conservative scholars, on the other hand, worry that Childs separates his theological reading of the OT from history. *See also* Childs, Brevard S.; form criticism (*Formgeschichte*); historical criticism; redaction criticism (*Redaktionsgeschichte*); source criticism.

carbon dating Carbon (or radiocarbon) dating is a tool used by archaeologists to date organic material found during the course of excavations. The principle is that if one can fix a date through carbon dating of some kind of organic material (wood, bone, etc.), then that will presumably fix the date of the particular stratum in which the material was found. Carbon contains a radioactive isotope (C-14) in the air that animals breathe and that plants take in through photosynthesis. During life the proportion of C-14 in the air is equal to that in the animal or plant, but upon death the C-14 in the latter begins to decay. Scientists know that the half-life of C-14 (the time it takes for half the C-14 to decay) is about 5,730 years, and so measuring the C-14 in organic material, typically by mass accelerator spectrometer, can help date it, give or take a range of years. Within the biblical period, C-14 dating cannot give a precise date, but it can determine the approximate time of the material under analysis. C-14 dating is typically only reliable for dates within the past fifty thousand years. *See also* archaeology.

casuistic law Apodictic law presents general ethical principles ("Do not murder," Exod. 20:13), while casuistic law applies these general ethical principles to specific cases. For instance, the goring-ox law (Exod. 21:28–32, 35–36) applies the law concerning murder to the case of a person's ox goring someone to death. There is extensive casuistic law in Exodus through Deuteronomy. *See also* apodictic law.

catechesis, catechetical Oral or sometimes written instruction in the basic doctrines of a religious faith. Certain books and passages in the Bible—such as Deuteronomy in the OT and Matthew in the NT—are often said to have been written to fulfill a catechetical role.

Catholic (or General) Epistles Designation given to the NT letters from James through Jude (James, 1 and 2 Peter; 1, 2, and 3 John; Jude). "Catholic" here means "universal" and comes from the fact that these letters seem to be written to general Christian audiences rather than to specific individuals or churches. The term is often used to distinguish these letters from the thirteen letters attributed to Paul, in which case Hebrews (when viewed as non-Pauline) could be listed among them.

CE *See* BCE/CE, BC/AD.

Chaldea, Chaldeans Chaldea refers to a region in southern Mesopotamia in the neo-Babylonian period (626–539 BC); the name Chaldeans refers to an Aramaic-speaking tribe that came to dominate that region, a tribe that then spread its sovereignty over all of Mesopotamia and into Syria-Palestine. Prominent kings of Babylon who were Chaldean include Nabopolassar (626–605 BC) and his son Nebuchadnezzar (605–562 BC). In a previous generation the Aramaic language was called Chaldean. *See also* Aram, Aramaic; Babylon.

charisma, charismatic From the Greek word *charisma*, "gift," referring to the spiritual gifts or empowerment bestowed by the Holy Spirit. The term "charismatic" can be used in various ways: (1) as a general adjective describing the gifts bestowed by the Spirit in the church; (2) of the Spirit-led nature of the early church, prior to the establishment of formal leadership offices, hierarchy, and institutional rules; (3) of one who believes in and practices the present-day manifestation of the so-called sign gifts, such as speaking in tongues, prophecy, healing, miracles, and so on.

chiasmus/chiasm A literary structure that forms a crossing pattern, which when outlined looks like the Greek letter chi (X), where the first part parallels the last part, the second part parallels the second to last part, and so on. This structure may be represented as follows (depending on how many units there are):

a b c d e [e′] d′ c′ b′ a′

The middle part (in this example represented by *e*) may have no parallel and thus stand out from the rest, perhaps as a point of emphasis. Chiasm can describe the structure of a single poetic line or of a whole discourse. *See also* parallelism; poetry.

Childs, Brevard S. (1923–2007) American Protestant OT professor who taught most of his career at Yale University. He is best known for his pronouncement that the biblical theology movement was dead and for his development of canonical criticism (or the canonical approach), though he himself did not like that term to describe his method. Childs wrote important commentaries on Exodus and Isaiah as well as introductions to both the OT and NT that demonstrated his distinctive approach to the interpretation of the biblical text. He was interested in recovering the OT for use in the church as well as the academy. Childs had tremendous influence on the next generation of OT scholarship, though he also had his critics. *See also* biblical theology movement; canonical criticism/approach.

chreia A term (pl.: *chreiai*) used in Greek rhetoric to refer to a short, pithy anecdote that reports a memorable saying or action of a prominent individual. The Greek word means "useful" and refers to the *chreia*'s function as a helpful teaching device. An example: "Alexander, the king of the Macedonians, was asked by someone where he kept his treasures, 'Here,' he said, pointing to his friends."[1] Many of Jesus's sayings in the Gospels could be identified as *chreiai*.

Christian Standard Bible (CSB) The Holman Christian Standard Bible (HCSB) is a new Bible version (not a revision) that originally released in 2004. A significantly revised edition came out in 2017 as the Christian Standard Bible (CSB). The (H)CSB was produced by the Sunday School Board of the Southern Baptist Convention and published by Broadman & Holman. The CSB is generally more literal than the NIV but less so than formal equivalent versions such as the New American Standard Bible (NASB) and the English Standard Version (ESV). According to its introduction, the CSB strives to balance formal and functional equivalence for "optimal equivalence." *See also* formal equivalent translation; functional equivalent translation.

christological/christotelic interpretation Refers to interpreting an OT passage as anticipating Christ. In Luke 24, Jesus twice tells his followers that all the Scriptures (at that time a reference to the OT) looked forward to his coming so that they were without excuse when they did not recognize him as the fulfillment of the OT hope (vv. 24–27, 44–45). Most christological/christotelic interpreters

---

1. Aelius Theon of Alexandria, *Exercises* 100, in *Progymnasmata: Greek Textbooks of Prose Composition and Rhetoric*, trans. George A. Kennedy (Leiden: Brill, 2003), 18.

recognize the importance of first interpreting an OT passage in its original setting before then interpreting it in the light of the coming of Christ. Some use the term "christological" as referring to the idea that the meaning of the OT passage's reference to Christ may be understood even before the coming of Christ, while christotelic interpreters argue that the deeper significance of the text is only revealed in the light of the death and resurrection of Christ.

Christology The field of Christian theology that examines the person and work of Jesus Christ.

Christophany A vision, appearance, or manifestation of Christ. The term is used of an appearance more glorious or supernatural than Jesus's daily interaction with his followers. NT Christophanies include the transfiguration (Mark 9:2–8 par.), the resurrection appearances (Matt. 28; Luke 24; John 20–21), and the appearance to Paul on the road to Damascus (Acts 9:3–16). OT manifestations of God in human form or the "angel of the LORD" (e.g., Gen. 18:1–33) are sometimes identified as Christophanies, though this is debated.

Chronicler The books of Chronicles are anonymous, so "the Chronicler" is a way to refer to their unknown final author(s). While we cannot identify the author(s) by name, we can date the final author to the postexilic period since the book refers to the return of the Jews after Cyrus's victory over the Babylonians and also because some of the genealogies (1 Chron. 1–9) extend many decades into the Persian period. We know that the Chronicler narrated the history of God's people in a way that spoke to their questions in the postexilic period, including (1) How are we connected to the past before the exile? and (2) How do we act now to please God?

Chrysostom, John (ca. 349–407) Early church father and archbishop of Constantinople. Chrysostom means "golden mouth" and was a nickname given because of his extraordinary eloquence and preaching skills. Chrysostom was also one of the most prolific authors in the early church.

Clement of Alexandria (ca. 150–215) Early Christian theologian who lived and taught in Alexandria, Egypt. The theologian Origen was one of his students. Clement was trained in Greek philosophy, especially Platonism and Stoicism, and sought to integrate these with a Christian worldview. The Alexandrian school was known for its allegorical interpretation of Scripture. Clement's main surviving works are a trilogy, *Protrepticus* (*Exhortation to the Greeks*), *Paedagogus* (*Christ the Educator*), and *Stromateis* (*Miscellanies*).

Clement of Rome (ca. 35–99) Early church leader and bishop of Rome from 88 to 99. He is sometimes referred to as Pope Clement I. His only authentic extant writing is *1 Clement*, a letter from the Christians in Rome to the Corinthian church. The letter asserts the authority of church leaders in response to insubordination by younger leaders in Corinth. The letter is traditionally included in the collection known as the Apostolic Fathers. A second letter, *2 Clement*, is today generally acknowledged to have been written by someone else. Clement is often called the first of the apostolic fathers. Tradition says he was martyred under the emperor Trajan in 99. *See also* apostolic fathers.

Clines, David J. A. (1938–) Australian biblical scholar who taught most of his career at the University of Sheffield and trained a number of doctoral students who are presently teaching at universities and seminaries around the world. He has also been influential through his numerous books and articles as well as his publishing ventures. In terms of his own research, Clines, who started his career as a relatively conservative exegete unpacking the meaning of the text, evolved into one of the most well-known postmodern interpreters of the end of the twentieth and beginning of the twenty-first centuries. He describes his approach as "bespoke criticism," using the analogy of the bespoke tailor, who cuts the cloth according to the specifications of the paying customer. Since the text has no "determinate meaning," the professional interpreter exegetes the text according to the specifications of the paying audience. In his very helpful Job commentary in the evangelical Word Biblical

Commentary, he provides a detailed historical-grammatical interpretation of the book, but in the preface he says he could have provided a feminist, Marxist, or vegetarian interpretation if he so chose. He reveals his Western liberal democratic sensibilities when he "reads against the grain" of texts that have violent or otherwise problematic elements in them. Clines also was one of the creators of the *Journal for the Study of the Old Testament* as well as Sheffield Academic Press, which has published the work of many other scholars.

codex A book-like document formed by folding papyrus sheets in half, laying one on top of another, and tying or gluing the sheets together. The codex replaced the scroll (a single sheet of papyrus rolled between two cylinders) during the Roman period. Whereas scrolls are generally written on only one side of the sheet, the sheets of a codex are written like a book, on both sides, making it a more efficient manner of recording text. *See also* scroll.

Codex Aleppo An important bound manuscript of the Hebrew Bible dating to the early tenth century AD, thus a little older than Codex Leningradensis. The Aleppo Codex had been preserved in full by the Jewish community in Aleppo, Syria, for five hundred years before it was removed for safekeeping after riots in 1947 over the establishment of a Jewish homeland in Palestine. A few years later when it resurfaced in Israel, it was missing parts, particularly a large part of the Torah. Like the later, yet fuller Codex Leningradensis, it was the work of the Masoretes. *See also* codex; Codex Leningradensis; Masoretes, Masoretic Text.

Codex Alexandrinus (A) A fifth-century uncial manuscript of the whole Greek Bible, identified with the siglum A (also numbered 02). It is one of four great uncial full-Bible manuscripts (LXX and NT), which also include Codex Sinaiticus (‭א‬), Codex Vaticanus (B), and Codex Ephraemi Rescriptus (C). Its name is derived from the fact that it was kept in Alexandria, Egypt, for a number of years until it was brought to Constantinople in the early seventeenth century. It was then given to Charles I of England and is currently housed in the British Library in London. The manuscript contains a nearly complete copy of the Septuagint, including a number of deuterocanonical books. The NT represents a mixed text type that is difficult to classify. The Gospels are closer to the Byzantine family (it is the oldest example of this family), while the rest of the NT is closer to the Alexandrian family. These differences raise significant questions about the legitimacy of traditional geographical textual-family classifications. *See also* codex; textual criticism; uncial.

Codex Bezae Cantabrigiensis (D) A fifth-century manuscript of the Greek NT, identified with the siglum D, containing, in both Greek and Latin, the text of the Gospels, the book of Acts, and a portion of 3 John. Codex Bezae is the most important example of the Western text type of the Greek NT. *See also* codex; textual criticism; uncial.

Codex Leningradensis The oldest extant complete manuscript of the Hebrew Bible, dated to AD 1009. It was produced by the Masoretes. Leningradensis (sometimes called Codex Furkowitz) is so named because it was the scroll of an ancient synagogue in St. Petersburg (named Leningrad during the Soviet period), Russia, and is now in a museum in that city. Leningradensis is the Hebrew text found in the body of the *Biblia Hebraica Stuttgartensia*, and thus is the standard Hebrew text used for modern translations and also for scholarly research. While by no means without textual problems (particularly in Samuel), Leningradensis is widely considered to be a reliable copy of the ancient Hebrew text. See also *Biblia Hebraica Stuttgartensia (BHS)*; codex; textual criticism.

Codex Sinaiticus (א) One of the earliest and most important Greek manuscripts of the Bible. It is one of four great uncial full-Bible manuscripts (LXX and NT), which also include Codex Alexandrinus (A), Codex Vaticanus (B), and Codex Ephraemi Rescriptus (C). Codex Sinaiticus was discovered in 1844 by Constantin von Tischendorf at St. Catherine's monastery on Mount Sinai. It is identified with the Hebrew siglum א (*aleph*). The manuscript dates from the mid-fourth century AD (ca. 330–60) and contains the Greek OT (the Septuagint), the Apocrypha, the NT, and two other early Christian writings—the *Epistle of Barnabas* and portions of the *Shepherd of Hermas*. About half of the OT has survived, and the whole of the NT and Apocrypha. Together with Codex Vaticanus, it is one of the earliest examples of the Alexandrian textual family. These two manuscripts were given great weight in the textual theories developed by B. F. Westcott and F. J. A. Hort, which became the foundation for modern text-critical studies of the NT. *See also* Apocrypha, the; codex; Codex Vaticanus (B); Septuagint; textual criticism; uncial; Westcott, Brooke Foss.

Codex Vaticanus (B)   One of the earliest Greek manuscripts of the Bible, Codex Vaticanus has been dated to the mid-fourth century. It is identified with the siglum B. It is one of four great uncial full-Bible manuscripts (LXX and NT), which also include Codex Alexandrinus (A), Codex Sinaiticus (א), and Codex Ephraemi Rescriptus (C). It has been kept in the Vatican library since at least the fifteenth century. The manuscript originally contained a nearly complete copy of the Greek OT (the Septuagint), the Apocrypha, and the NT. Today it is missing sections of Genesis, Psalms, 1 and 2 Timothy, Titus, Philemon, and Revelation. Together with Codex Sinaiticus, it is one of the earliest examples of the Alexandrian text family. These two manuscripts were given great weight in the textual theories developed by B. F. Westcott and F. J. A. Hort, which became the foundation for modern text-critical studies of the NT. *See also* codex; Codex Sinaiticus (א); Septuagint; textual criticism; uncial; Westcott, Brooke Foss.

colon, cola   Parallelism is a feature of Hebrew poetry. A parallel line is composed of two or three (and occasionally more) cola (the plural of colon) in which the second (and third) cola sharpen the thought of the first colon. A two-part parallel line is often called a bicolon:

> Why do the nations rage
>> and the peoples plot in vain? (Ps. 2:1)

A tricolon, on the other hand, is composed of three parts:

> How happy is the one
> who does not walk in the advice of the wicked
>> or stand in the pathway of sinners
>> or sit in the company of mockers. (Ps. 1:1)

See also parallelism; poetry.

Comma Johanneum *See* Johannine Comma.

Common English Bible (CEB) One of the more recent translations of the whole Bible into English, published in 2011. Its uniqueness lies in the fact that the translators include mainline as well as evangelical scholars. The translation is readable, having a balance between formal (word-for-word) and functional (thought-for-thought) translation philosophies. *See also* formal equivalent translation; functional equivalent translation.

Community Rule (1QS) One of the most important manuscripts discovered among the Dead Sea Scrolls. Previously referred to by scholars as the Manual of Discipline, the Community Rule (Heb.: *Serekh ha-Yahad*) describes rules and rituals related to the communal life for the sectarians who lived at the community at Qumran. *See also* Dead Sea Scrolls.

comparative/contextual method The OT was written in an ancient Near Eastern context. Particularly since the advent of the modern phase of archaeological study (starting around 1800) and the discovery of ancient texts written in Sumerian, Akkadian, Egyptian, Hittite, Ugaritic, Aramaic, and other less well-attested languages of the ancient Near East, scholars have studied the OT in the light of related ancient Near Eastern literature. The broad term for such study is the comparative method. In the history of the comparative method, there has been a tendency to overemphasize similarities, leading to what some have called "parallelomania," and this overemphasis then leads to some downplaying any significance to the ancient Near Eastern background of the text. W. W. Hallo of Yale University (1928–2015) proposed a middle way that found significance not only in similarities but also in the differences between biblical texts and analogues from other ancient Near Eastern cultures. Hallo had a profound influence on other scholars who are working today.

concordism The attempt to reconcile the Bible and science by seeing the Bible as expressing the insights of modern science using ancient language. Concordists, for instance, would argue that the sequence of creation in the six days in Genesis 1 reflects the actual order of creation. Some concordists believe that when the psalmist proclaims God as the one who "stretches out the heavens like a tent" (Ps. 104:2 NIV), this is a reference to the big bang theory of the origin of the universe. Critics of concordism argue that the Bible was written in a way that was understandable to its original audience and that did not embed references to modern science.

conditional sentence A sentence expressing the condition under which a particular action is achieved or fulfilled. A conditional sentence contains two parts, the *protasis* (the "if . . ." part) and the *apodosis* (the "then . . ." part). The apodosis is the main clause and the protasis is a subordinate clause. Example: "If you work hard [protasis], you will do well [apodosis]." There are four types of conditional clauses in Koine Greek: 1. *First-class conditions* ("conditions of fact") assume for the sake of the argument that if something is true, something else will follow: "If you live according to the flesh, you are going to die" (Rom. 8:13). 2. *Second-class conditions* ("contrary to fact") assume that if something were true (even though it is not), something else would follow: "If you believed Moses, you would believe me" (John 5:46). 3. *Third-class conditions* present a condition that might be true in the future or is generally true at all times: "But if her husband dies, she is free from that law" (Rom. 7:3). 4. *Fourth-class conditions* express a possible, usually remote, condition in the future. There are no complete examples in the NT (having both a protasis and an apodosis). Example: "Even if you should suffer because of righteousness, [you will be] blessed" (1 Pet. 3:14, authors' translation).

conflation The merging together of two or more sets of information. Mark's introductory OT quotation in Mark 1:2 is a conflation or combination of three texts: Isaiah 40:3; Malachi 3:1; and Exodus 23:20. The term is especially used in textual criticism to describe the scribal error of combining two readings found in different manuscripts. For example, some manuscripts of Romans 3:22 read that righteousness is given "to all who believe"; others read "in all who believe" (the Vulgate); and still others "in all and to all who believe." This third reading is likely a scribal conflation of the other two. Conflated readings are generally recognized as secondary, resulting from the scribal tendency to provide the fullest and most complete version of the text.

conflict story A category or "form" used in form-critical analysis of the Gospels to describe an episode in which Jesus comes into conflict with others, usually the religious leaders. Many conflict stories are also pronouncement stories, ending in an authoritative pronouncement by Jesus. Mark 2:1–3:6 is a series of five conflict stories, climaxing in a plot to take Jesus's life (3:6). *See also* form criticism (*Formgeschichte*); pronouncement story.

conquest, the Term used to refer to the entry of Israel under the leadership of Joshua into the promised land after their release from bondage in Egypt and forty years of wandering in the wilderness. The book of Joshua (chaps. 1–12) describes Israel's defeat of the previous inhabitants as a violent intrusion that first of all split the land in two by its defeats of the centrally located cities of Jericho and Ai and the problematic alliance with the Gibeonite confederacy.

This is followed by Joshua's defeat of a coalition of southern cities on the open battlefield and then the defeat of a northern coalition of cities. While one might get the impression from the first half of the book of Joshua that Israel completely subdued the native population, the description of the settlement (Josh. 13–24) and the opening of the book of Judges make it clear that Joshua's conquest was only the beginning of the conflict that ends only when David subdues Israel's final internal enemies. The date of the conquest, like the date of the exodus, is contested, with the leading contenders being the end of the fifteenth or the early fourteenth century over against a thirteenth-century date. Many dispute the historical accuracy of the conquest account due to what they believe are discrepancies with the archaeological record as well as what they interpret as conflicts within the biblical record. *See also* immigration model; minimalism; revolution model.

Contemporary English Version (CEV) An idiomatic and easy-to-read translation of the Bible produced under the auspices of the American Bible Society. The NT arose from a series of individual book translations produced by Barclay Newman. The NT was published in 1991 and the whole Bible in 1995. The preface to the CEV describes the version not as a replacement of other versions but as "a *companion*—the *mission* arm—of traditional translations." Special emphasis was also given to making the text clear and understandable for the public reading of Scripture.

Conzelmann, Hans (1915–89) German NT scholar who spent the bulk of his career as professor of NT at the University of Göttingen. Conzelmann had studied with Rudolf Bultmann and became one of the leading post-Bultmannians, who saw somewhat greater potential for discovering the historical Jesus than their mentor. His most influential work was *Die Mitte der Zeit* (The middle of time; English title: *The Theology of St. Luke*), in which he sought to apply the fledgling discipline of redaction criticism (*Redaktionge-schichte*) to Luke's two-volume work. Conzelmann claimed that, in light of the delay of the return of Christ (the parousia), Luke rewrote church history, transforming the church from an apocalyptic and charismatic community into an institutional one and pushing the eschaton into the distant future. *See also* Bultmann, Rudolf Karl; parousia; redaction criticism (*Redaktionsgeschichte*).

Council of Jamnia *See* Jamnia.

Council of Jerusalem Church gathering described in Acts 15, called to settle the dispute over whether Gentiles needed to be circumcised in order to be saved. According to the author of Acts, the council decided that, since both Jews and Gentiles were saved by grace, Gentiles should not be burdened with circumcision (15:11). The final verdict was rendered by James, leader of the Jerusalem church and half brother to Jesus (15:13–21). Though ruling against the necessity of circumcision, James stipulated that Gentiles should hold to certain standards of behavior, including abstaining from food polluted by idols, from sexual immorality, from eating the meat of strangled animals, and from blood (15:20). The precise nature and purpose of these standards is debated among scholars. According to Acts, the council drafted a letter that was then delivered to the Gentile churches of Antioch, Syria, and Cilicia.

Council of Nicaea (325) Also known as the First Council of Nicaea (a second Council of Nicaea was held in 787), this gathering was called by Emperor Constantine in 325 to settle the Arian controversy and other matters. It was held in the Bythian city of Nicaea (now Iznik, Turkey) and was the first ecumenical (worldwide) council of the early church. The most important result of the council was the establishment of the Nicene Creed, defining the nature of the Son of God and his relationship to God the Father. (The creed was amended at the First Council of Constantinople in 381.) The Council of Nicaea set a precedent for the establishment of uniform theology throughout the church. *See also* Arius, Arianism.

covenant English word commonly used to translate the Hebrew word *berit*. "Covenant" rightly captures the sense of the word as denoting a legal agreement between two parties. Recent research, however, has shown that a more specific type of legal agreement lies behind the word, namely a treaty between a great king and a vassal people (sometimes called a suzerainty treaty). Analogies have been recognized in particular between the structures of covenant passages like the book of Deuteronomy, Joshua 24, and 1 Samuel 12 on the one hand and Hittite vassal treaties from the middle of the second millennium BC on the other. Thus, when God enters a covenant with his people, he is the great king who enters a relationship with his servant people. At the heart of a covenant treaty is a historical prologue, which shows how good the sovereign has been toward the vassal in the past. Based on his past gracious acts, the sovereign then announces his law to the vassal, and these in turn are followed by blessings and curses dependent on obedience or disobedience, respectively. In the Bible the first named covenant is between God and Noah, which is a covenant with creation (Gen. 6:18; 9:9–17). While not called a covenant immediately, God's relationship with Abraham and the promises he makes to the patriarch are later referred to as a covenant (Gen. 12:1–3; 15:18; 17:2). God later enters a covenant with Israel through Moses as their leader at Mount Sinai (Exod. 24:7–8), a covenant that emphasizes law. Even later God confirms that David will be the first of a dynasty of kings (2 Sam. 7). At the end of the OT period, Israel so violates the covenant that God brings the kingship to an end, destroying Jerusalem and allowing the leading citizens of Judah to be exiled to Babylon. Jeremiah and other prophets announced this judgment as the consequence of Judah breaking the covenant and thus bringing on themselves the curses of the covenant. But Jeremiah looks beyond the judgment to the restoration and the onset of a "new covenant" (Jer. 31:31–34). This new covenant, which fulfills the old covenant, comes with Jesus, who instituted it at the Last Supper (Luke 22:20; see Heb. 8:7–13). *See also* Hatti.

criteria of authenticity A variety of criteria developed by scholars involved in historical-Jesus research for the purpose of discerning the authenticity of the words and actions of Jesus. Some of the most widely utilized criteria are as follows: (1) According to the *criterion of dissimilarity*, a saying or action of Jesus is considered authentic if it is dissimilar to the emphases of both Judaism and early Christianity. For example, Jesus's identification of himself as the "Son of Man" may be considered authentic since it was an unknown or uncommon messianic title in first-century Judaism and was not used as a title of worship in the early church. (2) The *criterion of multiple attestation* asserts that a saying or story is likely authentic if it appears in a multiplicity of Gospel sources. For example, Jesus's practice of eating with sinners appears in all strata of Gospel sources (according to the four-source theory [*see* Synoptic problem]), including Mark (Mark 2:15–17), Q (Matt. 11:18–19), Luke's special material ("L"; Luke 15:1–2), and Matthew's special material ("M"; Matt. 21:28–32). (3) The *criterion of Semitic flavor* states that a tradition that has a strong Palestinian flavor is more likely to be authentic. For example, Jesus's use of the Aramaic term *abba* ("father"; Mark 14:36) would be viewed as most likely authentic, since it arose in an Aramaic rather than Greek-speaking context. Over the years, the criteria have been subject to intense analysis, criticism, and scrutiny. Most Jesus scholars continue to use these and other criteria, though tailored to their own presuppositions, frameworks, and methods.

critical apparatus *See* apparatus, critical.

critical text A text of the Greek NT derived by following the standard rules of textual criticism and containing a critical apparatus citing variant readings. The two main editions of the critical text are the UBS (United Bible Societies) text, now in its fifth edition, and the Nestle-Aland text, now in its twenty-eighth edition (referred to by its [Latin] title, *Novum Testamentum Graece*, or by the initials NA followed by the edition number). The two were produced by the same committee and are identical except for some differences in punctuation and in their textual apparatus (the Nestle-Aland is more technical). *See also* apparatus, critical; textual criticism.

Crossan, John Dominic (1934–) Former priest and Irish American NT scholar whose research has focused especially on the historical Jesus. Together with Robert Funk, Crossan founded the controversial Jesus Seminar, which in the 1980s and '90s examined the historicity of the words and deeds of Jesus. Crossan identifies Jesus as a Cynic-like sage whose antihierarchical, egalitarian, and countercultural ideas resulted in his arrest and crucifixion. He rejects an eschatological Jesus in favor of one primarily opposed to the social structures of his day. *See also* Jesus Seminar.

Cullmann, Oscar (1902–99) German Lutheran theologian and NT scholar. Cullmann was most influential in biblical studies for his work in eschatology and Christology, developing a middle ground between the "imminent eschatology" of Albert Schweitzer and the "realized eschatology" of C. H. Dodd. Cullmann's view of "salvation history" (*Heilsgeschichte*) or "inaugurated eschatology" stressed Jesus as the center point of redemptive history. Against Rudolf Bultmann, who saw the NT as bearer of a message (kerygma) that must be understood in existential terms, Cullmann claimed the Bible bears witness to historical events that are the saving acts of God. These events lead up to the center point of time, which is the coming of Jesus. Salvation is achieved by what God does in history and not simply by acceptance of a message independent of history (see his *Christology of the New Testament*; *Christ and Time*; *Salvation in History*). Cullmann was also well known for his ecumenical efforts, building bridges of understanding between Protestant and Roman Catholic scholars and clergy. *See also* Bultmann, Rudolf Karl; *Heilsgeschichte*; Jeremias, Joachim; Ladd, George Eldon.

cult As used in biblical studies, "cult" refers to matters associated with formal religious worship. It is often used to describe ancient Israelite ritual such as priests, sacrifices, holy places (e.g., tabernacle and temple), and holy time (e.g., Sabbath).

cuneiform A form of writing. Meaning "wedge shaped," it refers to a system of symbols developed by Sumerians, then adapted by the Akkadians (and their descendants the Assyrians and Babylonians) to reflect their language. Others who used cuneiform writing include the inhabitants of ancient Ebla, the Hittites, and the Ugaritic-speaking inhabitants of what is today the coast of northern Syria. *See also* Akkadian; Eblaite; Hatti; Sumer; Ugaritic.

Cynic, Cynicism Philosophical movement commonly traced to Diogenes of Sinope (400–325 BC), who was known for his shrewd aphorisms and shocking behavior that challenged the cultural sensibilities of his day. Cynics were countercultural, wandering philosophers who rejected social norms. They typically dressed as beggars, with long hair and disheveled appearance, wearing a cloak and carrying a staff and a beggar's bag. The word "cynic" comes from the Greek word for "dog" and refers to Diogenes's outrageous public behavior, like using abusive language or performing public sexual acts. Though Cynics often reveled in shocking others, their primary goal was not to offend but to demonstrate a lifestyle unencumbered by social and cultural constraints. Some Jesus scholars—most famously John Dominic Crossan—have claimed that Jesus was a Cynic-like philosopher. He, like the Cynics, was a wandering itinerant whose clever aphorisms and parables challenged the social norms of his day. *See also* Crossan, John Dominic.

Cyrus Cylinder An eight-sided clay hollow cylinder, discovered in 1879, on which were written, in Akkadian, the deeds of Cyrus the Great (559–529 BC). In 539 BC Cyrus defeated the Babylonian Empire and thus inherited its vast territory, including the province of Yehud (Judah) with its capital at Jerusalem. According to 2 Chronicles 36:22–23 and Ezra 1:1–4, Cyrus issued a decree that allowed Jews who had been exiled by the Babylonians to return to their homeland and rebuild their temple in Jerusalem. The Cyrus Cylinder is particularly interesting for biblical studies since it gives a broader Persian perspective on this decree. The cylinder describes how Cyrus encouraged all of Babylon's vassals—the Jewish people are not specifically named—to return to their homelands and restore their sacred sites. This action was part of Persia's efforts to create cooperative vassal states that would serve Persian interests. The biblical perspective is that God used this foreign policy for his own purposes. *See also* Akkadian; Babylon; Persia; postexilic period.

D

D *See* Codex Bezae Cantabrigiensis (D).

Damascus Document The only document associated with the Dead Sea Scrolls that was known before their discovery in 1946–56. A number of fragments of the Damascus Document were discovered by Solomon Schechter in 1897 in the Cairo Genizah (a genizah is a storeroom for old documents), adjoining the Ben Ezra Synagogue in old Cairo, Egypt. These documents were originally called the Zadokite fragments because of references in them to the sons of Zadok the priest. The documents contain moral instruction, exhortation, warnings, and legal material for a covenant community. A figure known as the Teacher of Righteousness plays a prominent role in this community. When the Dead Sea Scrolls were discovered starting in 1946, scholars recognized that some of the scrolls matched the Zadokite fragments. The fragments were subsequently renamed the Damascus Document because of numerous references in them to Damascus. Scholars debate whether this refers to the literal city of Damascus in Syria or whether it is a code word for something else, perhaps the community at Qumran itself. *See also* Dead Sea Scrolls; genizah.

Dead Sea Scrolls Between 1946 and 1956 hundreds of fragments and even full texts were discovered in eleven caves on the northwest coast of the Dead Sea, thirty miles from Jerusalem, near the archaeological site of Khirbet Qumran, which is thought to be the location of the community that used these texts. These texts may be dated between the third century BC and the first century AD. The Dead Sea Scrolls include many biblical texts; indeed every book of the OT is attested from the caves with the exception of Esther. Among the greatest finds were nearly complete copies of Isaiah and Psalms. There are also a great number of extrabiblical writings, including commentaries and sectarian writings. Among the most famous of these are the Community Rule (1QS), the War Scroll (1QM), Thanksgiving Hymns (1QH), the Temple Scroll (11Q19), and the Copper Scroll (3Q15). In the siglum identifying each scroll, "Q" stands for "Qumran," and the number before it indicates the cave in which the scroll was found (documents have been discovered in 11 caves). The biblical texts found at the Dead Sea demonstrated that the Hebrew text had not yet been standardized into a single text type; they also demonstrated, by virtue of a number of texts' similarity to the Codex Leningradensis, dating to about a millennium later (AD 1009), that reliable transmission of the biblical text over a long time was possible.

The scrolls suggest that the community at Qumran arose from a group of priests descended from Zadok, who rejected the present Jerusalem priesthood and withdrew to the Judean wilderness. The Qumran sectarians were led by a charismatic figure known as the Teacher of Righteousness, who had been persecuted by a Jerusalem high priest, identified in the scrolls as the "Wicked Priest."

The Qumran community was eschatological in its perspective, viewing themselves as the "true Israel" and expecting the soon end of the age. Using what has been called a *pesher* method of interpretation, they applied biblical prophecies to their own situation. In a coming war against the Romans, they expected to join with God's angels for a great victory over the forces of darkness. The group anticipated two messiahs, or "anointed ones," a royal messiah descended from David and a priestly messiah from the line of Aaron. Though their fate is shrouded in mystery, the Qumran community was likely wiped out by the Romans in the Jewish revolt of AD 66–74. *See also* Community Rule (1QS); Damascus Document; Essenes.

Decalogue God delivered the law to Moses on Mount Sinai beginning with ten statements of general ethical principles (Exod. 20:2–17; Deut. 5:6–21). Though commonly known as the Ten Commandments, they are referred to in the Bible as the "Ten Words" or "Ten Statements" (Exod. 34:28), which is the meaning of the English word "Decalogue." *See also* apodictic law.

deconstruction A school of thought associated with Jacques Derrida, who achieved prominence in literary theory during the 1970s through the '90s, influencing a number of different biblical interpreters during that period (most notably D. J. A. Clines). The basic premise of deconstruction is that there is no determinate meaning of a biblical text. Thus, the biblical interpreter notes how the text undermines its own message. For instance, one study showed that the David and Goliath story, while on one level attributing David's victory over Goliath to God, also describes David as using human craftiness and skill (the use of a slingshot rather than a sword) to win. Others, like Clines, suggest that since the text has no determinate meaning, the professional interpreter can create whatever meaning they desire to meet the needs of those who commission them to interpret the text. Derrida's influence on biblical studies has been on the wane since the turn of the century. *See also* Clines, David J. A.

Deir 'Alla inscription Discovered in 1967 and published for the first time in 1976, this inscription is important because it mentions the non-Israelite prophet Balaam, known from Numbers 22–24. The inscription was written with ink on plaster walls and dates to around 800 BC; it was found in pieces in Deir 'Alla, a site about six miles east of the Jordan River in an area known as Gilead, which was at that time occupied by Israelites. The text relates that Balaam received a vision from the gods that portended darkness and misery. Parts of the text are difficult to understand.

Deissmann, Gustaf Adolf (1886–1937) German Protestant theologian and biblical scholar best known for his work in ancient Near Eastern studies and the Greek of the NT. Using the papyri documents discovered in Egypt, Deissmann demonstrated that the NT was written in the *koinē*, or the common Greek of the Hellenistic world, rather than a special "Holy Ghost" language unique to the Scriptures (see *Light from the Ancient East: The New Testament Illustrated by Recently Discovered Texts of the Graeco-Roman World* [London: Hodder & Stoughton, 1910]). Deissmann also worked ecumenically for peace between nations and was twice nominated for the Nobel Peace Prize.

delay of the parousia *See* Conzelmann, Hans; parousia.

demythologization *See* Bultmann, Rudolf Karl.

deuterocanonical *See* Apocrypha, the.

Deuteronomic/Deuteronomistic History A term often used to describe the history given in Joshua through Kings in contrast to the history presented in the books of Chronicles. Scholars often suggest that the different tone of Joshua through Kings (particularly Samuel and Kings) is the result of the fact that the final form of these books was completed during the exile and sought to answer the question, Why are we in exile? Thus, the history of Israel and that of Judah are presented through the lens of the book of Deuteronomy, showing how God's people violated the covenant and in particular the distinctive laws of Deuteronomy (*see* Deuteronomistic) and that they are thus suffering in exile because the Deuteronomic curses threatening defeat and exile have come into effect (see in particular Deut. 28:25–29, 37–38, 49–68). *See also* Chronicler.

Deuteronomistic The book of Deuteronomy has a distinctive theology, and when its influence is detected in other biblical books, they are often designated as Deuteronomistic. This distinctive theology includes an emphasis on the centralization of sacrificial worship (Deut. 12), instructions on being a godly king (17:14–20), the difference between true and false prophets (13:1–11; 18:14–22), and the curses and rewards that are consequences for one's obedience or lack of obedience of the law (chaps. 27–28). The prophet Jeremiah is often considered an example of a Deuteronomistic thinker, particularly in how he accuses Judah of breaking the law and thus threatens them with the curses of the covenant.

deutero-Pauline Term used to describe letters attributed to Paul but viewed by many scholars as written pseudonymously in Paul's name. "Deutero" means "second" and refers to a secondary author writing in Paul's name. The letters most widely viewed as deutero-Pauline are the Pastoral Epistles (1 and 2 Timothy and Titus). Other disputed letters include Ephesians, Colossians, Philemon, and 2 Thessalonians.

Dever, William (1933–) American archaeologist who spent most of his teaching career at the University of Arizona, establishing one of the most influential graduate programs in archaeology for the study of the ancient Near East. He was an active field archaeologist, most notably at Gezer. At the beginning of his career, Dever argued that archaeology in the Near East should be known not as biblical archaeology but rather as Syro-Palestinian archaeology in order to avoid the idea that archaeology in the region was only in the service of the Bible. Dever helped develop what came to be called the "internal transformation" model of Israel's emergence in the land. He links his hypothesis to the observation that about three hundred small sites with similar technologies (plaster-lined cisterns for collecting water, olive grove terracing) spring up at the beginning of the Iron Age (ca. 1200 BC) just as large Canaanite coastal cities are collapsing. He is especially drawn to the absence of pig bones at the sites, which may suggest a people, like the Hebrews, who did not eat pork. Dever grew up in a conservative Protestant setting but has distanced himself from it, though he is also critical of minimalism. *See also* internal transformation model; minimalism.

diachronic, synchronic "Diachrony" comes from a Greek phrase that translates roughly as "through time" and refers to an analysis that considers the relationship between earlier and later texts or studies the development of a text through time. The Documentary Hypothesis, for instance, speculates that the Pentateuch as we know it developed over time by a combination of various sources over centuries. A synchronic analysis does not ask about relative dating but rather simply studies a text or a biblical book as it presently stands. These terms are also used in lexicography, the study of words. Diachronic word studies examine how word meanings change over time, while synchronic studies examine the semantic range of words at a particular point in time.

dialogical analysis Emanating from the work of the Russian philosopher Mikhail Bakhtin (1895–1975), dialogic analysis looks at literary or spoken communication as an interaction not only with previous literature but also with literature to be written in the future. In regard to biblical studies, it is a kind of intertextual analysis of the type that attends to the echoes of earlier literature but also reads a text in the light of literature written afterward. Dialogical analysis does not seek resolution but allows for continuing tension between perspectives.

diaspora Term meaning "dispersion" and referring to Jews living outside the land of Israel. Jews were dispersed both because of forced exile, as in the Babylonian exile, and for economic reasons, as when Jacob took his family to Egypt (Gen. 47:4). By the first century there were Jewish communities and synagogues throughout the Mediterranean world. James writes his letter "to the twelve tribes dispersed abroad" (James 1:1). This is probably a reference to Jewish Christians who were scattered outside of Israel because of persecution. *See also* postexilic period.

Diatessaron Early Christian harmony of the four Gospels produced by the church father Tatian around AD 170. *Diatessaron* means "through (the) four (Gospels)." Tatian did not place the four Gospels in parallel columns, as most modern harmonies and synopses, but instead brought them together into one continuous story. Where there were apparent inconsistencies, he chose one Gospel's account or added harmonizing details. Rather than following one Gospel's order, he created his own narrative sequence. The *Diatessaron* was widely used throughout the church and became the official lectionary for the Gospels in some Syriac-speaking churches until the fifth century. It is debated whether the *Diatessaron* was originally composed in Syriac or in Greek.

diatribe Whereas today a "diatribe" is a harangue or forceful verbal attack against someone or something, in Greco-Roman literature the term referred to a brief speech or dialogue intended to exhort or persuade with reference to a particular social, ethical, or moral issue. Diatribes often entailed a conversation with an imaginary opponent and/or a response to a rhetorical question. Sections of Paul's Letters, especially Romans, have been compared to Greco-Roman diatribe.

Didache An anonymous document known in ancient times as *The Teaching of the Lord to the Gentiles by the Twelve Apostles*, or *The Teaching of the (Twelve) Apostles*. The *Didache* (Gk. for "teaching") is one of the earliest postapostolic writings, dated by most scholars to the late first century. Its traditions may go back even earlier, to the mid-first century. Although the book was known by title from various ancient sources, no copy was available in modern times until 1873, when Philotheos Bryennios discovered a manuscript that contained the full text of the *Didache* in Greek. The *Didache* has three sections. The first deals with the "two ways" of life and death and may have originally been adapted from a Jewish work (1:1–6:2). The second section deals with various church practices and functions, such as food, baptism, fasting, prayer, the Eucharist, and leadership roles in the church (6:3–16:2). The third section is a very brief apocalyptic passage (16:3–8). Some passages show similarity to canonical texts, especially passages from the Gospel of Matthew.

discourse analysis A variety of linguistic methods and approaches that move beyond analysis of the sentence to that of the discourse as a whole. It is also known as text-linguistics, though text-linguistics is sometimes viewed as a subdiscipline within discourse analysis.

dispensationalism A theological system that claims God works in distinct ways with different groups of people in different periods or ages ("dispensations") of history. Dispensationalism is generally contrasted with covenant theology, which stresses the continuity between Israel and the church (identified as the "new Israel"). Dispensationalism, by contrast, stresses discontinuity, with Israel and the church having different roles and purposes in God's plan. The nature and number of dispensations varies among interpreters, but the traditional seven dispensations are (1) innocence (Adam to fall), (2) conscience (fall to flood), (3) government (flood to Babel), (4) promise (Abraham to Moses), (5) law (Moses to the cross), (6) grace (the cross to the rapture), and (7) millennial kingdom (one thousand years from the second coming to the new heaven and earth). Each dispensation moves through a cycle of (1) God's revelation of standards of behavior, (2) human rebellion and rejection, (3) God's judgment followed by a new dispensation.

Dispensationalism was developed especially by John Nelson Darby (1800–1882) and popularized by C. I. Scofield in the Scofield Reference Bible. Today dispensationalism takes a variety of forms, usually identified as classical (Darby; Scofield), traditional (J. Walvoord; C. Ryrie), and progressive (D. Bock; C. Blaising; R. Saucy). Classical and traditional dispensationalists continue to see a strict distinction between Israel and the church. They see an essential role for the modern state of Israel and argue for a pretribulational rapture of the church. The church (the dispensation of grace) must be removed from earth before God can turn again to deal with the nation of Israel. The seven-year tribulation period, the rise of the antichrist, and the second coming represent a return to and completion of the dispensation of law (= Daniel's seventieth week; Dan. 9). Progressive dispensationalism, developed in the

1990s, sees significantly more continuity between Israel and the church and thus occupies a middle ground between traditional dispensationalism and covenant theology. *See also* premillennialism; rapture; tribulation period.

dissimilarity, criterion of *See* criteria of authenticity.

dittography *See* haplography.

divided monarchy Upon the death of Solomon (928 BC), his son Rehoboam immediately assumed the throne in Judah, but he then traveled north to receive the acclamation of the northern tribes (1 Kings 12). Rather than agreeing to soften his father's policy toward the northern tribes, he agreed to his younger advisers' counsel to intensify the northern tribes' obligations to the throne. They promptly withdrew their support and appointed Jeroboam as their king, thus splitting the kingdom of Israel into two parts and initiating the period known as the divided monarchy. The northern tribes were eventually defeated by the Assyrians, and their land was incorporated as a province into the vast Assyrian Empire (722 BC). The Assyrians deported some of the northern kingdom's citizens and also imported foreigners into the region; thus the northern kingdom was never restored. The south continued to be ruled by a descendant of David until it too was conquered (586 BC), this time by Babylon, which had earlier defeated Assyria and inherited its lands. The Babylonians deported the elites but did not introduce foreign elements into the land. The Babylonians brought the monarchy to an end.

divine council In the ancient Near East, the divine realm was thought to be populated by many gods and goddesses. While some were more powerful than others and there were conflicts among the gods, they are sometimes imagined as meeting together to make decisions. For instance, at the beginning of the Ugaritic Baal Myth, Yam sends two messengers to the divine council to assert his kingship and demand that Baal be made his slave. They signal that they are ready to acquiesce to Yam's demand, but Baal spits into their midst, storms out of the council, and prepares to fight Yam. In the Bible, we get occasional descriptions of God meeting with a heavenly council, but in the case of the Bible the members of the council are angels. For instance, Job 1 pictures God meeting with the angelic council. Psalm 82 depicts God addressing the "great assembly" composed of "gods" (here used to refer to angels). The divine council is almost certainly in mind when God speaks in the first-person plural as he prepares to create humanity ("Let us make . . . ," Gen. 1:26) and when he announces judgment against those who build the Tower of Babel ("Let's go down there and confuse their language," Gen. 11:7).

divine man (*theios anēr*) A designation first introduced by Richard Reitzenstein (1861–1931), German classical philologist and scholar of ancient Greek religion and gnosticism, with reference to a class of the Hellenistic preachers and miracle workers. Examples of such "divine men" include Apollonius of Tyana and the seer and religious founder Alexander of Abonoteichus. In the literature such men are sometimes considered capable of knowing the future in advance, healing the sick, or even raising the dead. In the history of religions school (*Religionsgeschichtliche Schule*) in particular, the miracle stories about Jesus and titles such as Son of God are sometimes said to be influenced by such divine-man narratives. *See also* Bousset, Wilhelm; history of religions school (*Religionsgeschichtliche Schule*).

Divine Warrior After the crossing of the Red (or Reed) Sea, Moses sings, "The Lord is a warrior" (Exod. 15:3). In numerous places in the OT, the biblical authors depict God as a warrior who enters the battle, typically on behalf of his people, but also, when they are disobedient, against them as well. Before the battle of Jericho, Joshua encounters the Divine Warrior, who has taken human form and stands with a drawn sword (Josh. 5:13–15). At the end of the OT time period, when Judah no longer has a king and is not an independent nation-state, the prophets deliver oracles announcing the future intervention of God the warrior (Dan. 7 and

Zech. 14). In the NT Jesus is the Divine Warrior who transforms warfare from that focused on human enemies to war "against the rulers, against the authorities, against the cosmic powers of this darkness, against evil, spiritual forces in the heavens" (Eph. 6:12). In the future, however, at Jesus's second coming, he will return to wage war against all human and spiritual enemies (Rev. 19:11–21).

docetism Early Christian doctrine, deemed heretical by the church, that claimed Jesus only appeared to have a physical body but was in fact pure spirit (Gk. *dokeō* means "to seem" or "to appear"). Many docetists were also gnostics. Docetism rejects the true incarnation of the Son of God and—since he is not truly human—his suffering as an atoning sacrifice for sins. For some docetists, such as the gnostic Marcion, Jesus was fully divine and his body was only apparent, a phantom. Others, such as Cerinthus, distinguished the man Jesus from the Christ Spirit. Cerinthus, who was purported to be an opponent of the apostle John at Ephesus, claimed the Christ Spirit came upon Jesus at his baptism and abandoned him prior to his crucifixion. The letter of 1 John may have been written in part against this version of docetism. Docetism was rejected by the church at the First Council of Nicaea in 325 and is deemed heretical by all major wings of the Christian church, including Roman Catholic, Orthodox, and Protestant denominations. *See also* gnosticism, *gnōsis*.

Documentary Hypothesis The Documentary Hypothesis (DH) is a particular view of the composition of the Pentateuch as determined through a source-critical analysis. Sometimes it is called Wellhausianism, since its popularizer was Julius Wellhausen, whose work at the end of the nineteenth century remains extremely influential. Wellhausen was not the first to develop a theory of sources of the Pentateuch. Such speculation had been going on at least since the end of the seventeenth century, but Wellhausen expressed his conclusions in a way that influenced not only European and British scholars but also the vast majority of American scholars at the end of the nineteenth and the beginning of the twentieth centuries. Many still hold a version of the DH today.

The DH explains the Pentateuch as the result of a combining of four previous independent sources that came from different time periods and regions of Israel and were combined over time by redactors to produce the Pentateuch as we know it. As developed by Wellhausen and those who followed him, this removes the production of the Pentateuch from Moses, who is the traditional author, though he is never named as such within the Pentateuch itself.

Four main criteria are used to separate the now-joined sources. These include the presence of the divine names Yahweh and Elohim, double namings (for instance Mount Sinai is sometimes called Mount Horeb), double stories (notice the two creation accounts in Gen. 1 and 2), and, finally, different theologies (for example, some texts presume multiple altars, others mandate a single altar, and still others presuppose a single altar).

These criteria lead many to differentiate four sources. The oldest source (J) uses the divine name Yahweh (Jahwe in the German); thus the term Yahwist/Jahwist refers to the anonymous composer(s) of this source. The other sources refer to God as Elohim. Indeed, the second-oldest source is often identified as E, for Elohist. J was dated by Wellhausen to the tenth century BC and purported to be written in the south of Israel, while E was written in the north and from the ninth century. Some scholars today believe that the distinctions between J and E are so minimal as not to warrant positing an E source. The third source is connected to the distinctive theology of the book of Deuteronomy (D, the Deuteronomist) and is dated to the seventh century BC, while the Priestly source (P) is dated to the exilic or postexilic period. *See also* source criticism; Wellhausen, Julius.

Dodd, Charles Harold (1884–1973) Influential Welsh NT scholar who taught at the Universities of Oxford (1915–30), Manchester (1930–35), and Cambridge, becoming emeritus there in 1949. Dodd is most famous for popularizing the perspective of "realized eschatology," meaning that the kingdom Jesus announced and inaugurated was a present spiritual reality rather than a future (apocalyptic) hope. *See also* Cullmann, Oscar; Ladd, George Eldon.

dominical saying From the Latin *dominus*, meaning "lord" or "master," a saying or teaching attributed to Jesus Christ. The term is often used in historical-Jesus studies for an authentic saying of Jesus as opposed to one that is considered to be the creation of the early church.

Douay Bible An English version of the Bible translated from the Latin Vulgate, authorized by the Roman Catholic Church. It is also known as the Douay-Rheims Bible. The NT was published in Reims, France, in 1582, and the rest of the Bible with Apocrypha at the University of Douai in 1609 and 1610. The primary impetus for the version was to uphold Catholic doctrine in the face of the rising Protestant movement. The version had extensive marginal notes dealing with issues of translation and defending Catholic and patristic theology. *See also* Apocrypha, the.

doublet Two different but similar episodes that are sometimes said to have arisen from a single original story. Possible examples in the OT include the two creation accounts (Gen. 1–2) and two episodes where Abraham tries to pass off his wife, Sarah, as his sister (Gen. 12:10–20; 20:1–18). His son Isaac later tries to do the same thing (Gen. 26:6–11). Examples in the NT Gospels include Matthew's two accounts of the healing of two blind men (Matt. 9:27–31; 20:29–34) and Mark's (and Matthew's) two miracles of multiplying bread and fishes—the feeding of the five thousand and the four thousand (Mark 6:32–44; 8:1–10; cf. Matt. 14:13–21; 15:32–39). The claim is often made by form critics that the Gospel writers mistakenly treated two versions of the same story as different historical events. *See also* Documentary Hypothesis; source criticism.

double tradition *See* Synoptic problem.

E

Ea, Enki Ea is the Akkadian (Babylonian/Assyrian) and Enki is the Sumerian name for one of the most important gods in the Mesopotamian pantheon. He is the god of wisdom and plays a role in many important myths. For biblical studies, he is best known for the role he plays in the creation texts, particularly Enuma Elish and Atrahasis. This god is not specifically mentioned in the Bible. *See also* Atrahasis; Enuma Elish.

Ebla *See* Eblaite.

Eblaite In the late 1970s during excavations of Tell Mardikh (near Aleppo in Syria) a number of cuneiform tablets were discovered dating to 2500 to 2250 BC. While most of these tablets were written in Sumerian, a number were written in a hitherto unknown Northwest Semitic language (like Hebrew, Ugaritic, and Aramaic). When first discovered, the Ebla tablets showed great promise for illuminating biblical language, customs, literary genres, and more. However, for political (the tablets are largely housed in war zones in Syria) and other reasons, the study of these tablets has been slow. Their potential for the study of the OT is thus yet to be determined. *See also* Aram, Aramaic; cuneiform; Hebrew language; Sumer; Ugaritic.

Edom A nation-state located to the south and southeast of Judah during the biblical period. The Bible places its roots in Jacob's brother Esau (whose other name was Edom, "red") and his descendants (Gen. 36). Israel and Edom found themselves in conflict from time to time (Num. 20:14–21; 2 Sam. 8:14; 2 Kings 8:20). In the aftermath of the Babylonian defeat of Jerusalem, the biblical authors express anger toward the treatment Judah received from the Edomites (Ps. 137:7; Lam. 4:22; Ezek. 35:15; Obad. 10–14).

Egypt One of the earliest civilizations and nation-states in human history, Egypt is located on both banks of the Nile River, whose annual flooding, extended by irrigation, covered the valley with arable soil whose crops sustained its population. The history of Egypt began with the union of Upper (southern) and Lower (northern) Egypt under a single pharaoh in the thirty-first century BC. After an "Early Dynastic Period," the history of Egypt is divided into three periods of centralized government (Old [2686–2180 BC], Middle [2133–1670 BC], and New [1570–709 BC] Kingdoms), interrupted by two periods of relative weakness and political fragmentation (First [2180–2133 BC] and Second [1670–1570 BC] Intermediate Periods). There followed a Late Period (750–343 BC). The Greek king Alexander (the Great) was made pharaoh in 331 BC. Eventually, after his death, his general Ptolemy I assumed leadership and established a dynasty that lasted until 30 BC. At that time, after defeating his rival Mark Antony and Egypt's Queen Cleopatra VII in battle, Octavian (Caesar Augustus) annexed the Ptolemaic kingdom of Egypt for Rome. It remained a Roman province throughout the NT period.

Egypt first appears in biblical history when Abraham and Sarah go there to seek help during a famine (Gen. 12:10–20) and then appears numerous times afterward. The date of the Israelite exodus from Egypt is debated, but it is associated with the New Kingdom period. The Bible and extrabiblical texts also record Pharaoh Neco II's (610–595 BC) attempt to bolster the Assyrian army over against a growing Babylonian threat. On the way up to the battle in northern Syria, King Josiah of Judah (639–609 BC) lost his life trying to prevent Neco from reaching the Assyrians (2 Kings 23:29–30), and on the way back Neco meddled with the succession in Judah, removing one son of Josiah (Jehoahaz) and placing a more cooperative son (Jehoiakim) on the throne instead (2 Kings 23:31–37). Daniel 11 prophetically describes the conflict between Egyptian Ptolemaic kings (kings "of the south") and Seleucid kings (kings "of the north"). *See also* hieroglyphics.

Egyptian language *See* hieroglyphics.

Eichrodt, Walther (1890–1978) One of the most influential OT theologians of the mid-twentieth century, whose impact continues to the present day. A German Protestant thinker, his monumental *Theology of the Old Testament,* first published in Germany between 1933 and 1935, directed the next generations of scholars toward the pivotal importance of the covenant for the theology of the OT. He divided his work into a study of the relationship between covenant and the world and covenant and man. He wrote other books and articles, notably an important commentary on Ezekiel for the Old Testament Library. He taught at the University of Basel (overlapping with the theologian Karl Barth) from 1922 to 1960. *See also* covenant.

Eighteen Benedictions *See* Shemoneh Esreh (Eighteen Benedictions).

eisegesis From Greek, "bring into." A pejorative technical term that is the counterpart to "exegesis." Whereas "exegesis" means "a drawing out" of the original author's intended meaning, "eisegesis" means "a bringing into" or imposing of the interpreter's own (biased) interpretation on the text. The term is most commonly used in evangelical settings. *See also* exegesis.

Eissfeldt, Otto (1887–1973) German Protestant OT scholar who taught for the bulk of his career at the University of Halle-Wittenberg. He specialized in literary-critical analyses of the biblical text following in the lines of Julius Wellhausen and Eissfeldt's teacher, Hermann Gunkel. Eissfeldt is best known today for *The Old Testament: An Introduction,* which was first published in German in 1934. *See also* Gunkel, Hermann; Wellhausen, Julius.

ekklēsia   Greek term most commonly translated "church" but with a range of meanings that include "assembly," "gathering," and "congregation." It is the term Jesus uses in Matthew 16:18, when he identifies Peter as the rock upon which Jesus's "church" will be built. It can refer to a single local congregation (Rom. 16:5: "the church that meets in their home"), a group of related house churches in a larger city (1 Cor. 1:2: "the church of God at Corinth"), or the worldwide body of believers, the church universal (Eph. 5:25: "Husbands, love your wives, just as Christ loved the church and gave himself for her").

Ekron   City located inland in the north of Philistine territory. After the Philistines captured the ark at the end of Eli's judgeship, they first put it in the temple of their god Dagon in Ashdod, then in Gath, but both places suffered horrific consequences. When the people of Gath sent the ark to Ekron, Ekron sent it back to Israel out of fear (1 Sam. 5–6). King Ahaziah brought on God's judgment as announced by the prophet Elijah when he consulted the god of Ekron, referred to as Baal-Zebub (2 Kings 1). Baal-Zebub, which means "lord of the flies," is likely a pejorative name for a deity who had the name Baal-Zebul, which means "lord, the prince." *See also* Ashdod; Ashkelon; Gath; Gaza; Philistia.

El   A Northwest Semitic name that means simply "god." In Ugaritic texts that reflect Canaanite religious ideas, El is the father of Baal. In the Baal Myth, Baal must seek his father's permission to build his house, and El is forced to give his permission by the threats of his daughters Asherah and Anat. Later when Baal dies (swallowed by the god of death), El cuts himself in what appears to be a mourning ritual. While El is the nominal head of the pantheon, he does not seem to be a very imposing figure in the myths. In the Bible, while sometimes El should simply be translated "god," other occurrences refer specially to Israel's God, sometimes in combination with other elements like *El Elohe Israel* ("God, the God of Israel"; Gen. 33:20). Some scholars propose that Israel's concept of God grew out of the Canaanites' understanding of the god El, but this idea is out of keeping with the Bible's own distinction between Israel's God and the Canaanite gods. *See also* Asherah; Baal; Baal texts; Ugaritic.

Elephantine texts   Elephantine was an island and the location of a Jewish mercenary colony located in the Aswan region in Egypt at the end of the fifth century BC. About 175 papyrus documents of many different types (including business documents, legal documents, letters, and divorce proceedings), written in Aramaic, have been discovered at the site. Two texts having significance for the study of the OT include (1) the Passover letter, often dated to 419 BC and giving instructions for the observance of Passover; and (2) a letter to the Persian-appointed governor of Judah, Bagoas, that has to do with the rebuilding of the community's temple. In 410 BC their temple was destroyed by native Egyptians under the leadership of a local priest of the god Chnum. The Jewish community asked for permission to rebuild, which they were given, but they were not given permission to offer animal sacrifices (likely in keeping with the so-called law of centralization; Deut. 12). The letter also mentions Sanballat the governor of Samaria, who is mentioned in the book of Nehemiah. *See also* Aram, Aramaic.

ellipsis   Literary term for the omission of a word or phrase where it might be expected. In biblical studies, the term is used in the analysis of a poetic line where, in order to achieve terseness, the second and (if present) third cola often omit an element of the first colon. In Psalm 2:8 we note that the verb ("I will make") only occurs in the first colon but is understood in the second.

> I will make the nations your inheritance
> and the ends of the earth your possession.

See also colon, cola; parallelism; poetry; terseness.

Elohist   In the Documentary Hypothesis, Elohist is the name given to the anonymous author of one of the four sources that were woven together by redactors in order to create the final Torah or Pentateuch. The Elohist source (E) is named by virtue of the fact that it uses the term *'elohim* rather than Yahweh (in German, Jahwe, thus the source J) to refer to the God of Israel. While J was thought to originate in southern Israel in the tenth century BC, E is said to be a product of northern tribes in the ninth century BC. Today many scholars who advocate the Documentary Hypothesis are skeptical about a separate E source. *See also* Documentary Hypothesis.

emendation   Term associated with textual criticism, involving the judgment that the Hebrew or Greek text contains additions to or omissions from the original text (autograph) that must be changed (emended) in order to restore the text. *See also* autograph; textual criticism.

English Standard Version (ESV)   A revision of the Revised Standard Version (RSV) published by Crossway Books in 2001. The ESV modified the RSV text in a more conservative direction, for example, by replacing "young woman" with "virgin" in Isaiah 7:14 and "expiation" with "propitiation" in Romans 3:25. The ESV preface asserts that the version renders the text in an "essentially literal" (formal equivalence) fashion. *See also* formal equivalent translation.

Enkidu   A major character in the Gilgamesh Epic. At the beginning of the story, Gilgamesh is a young king of the city of Uruk, and his immature leadership is a problem for the city's inhabitants, who pray to the gods to help them. The gods respond by creating Enkidu, a primal man who appears in the wilderness. Lured into the city by a prostitute, Enkidu fights Gilgamesh. Though it is a close match, Gilgamesh defeats him. The experience, though, leads the two to form a friendship, and they embark on adventures, thus solving the citizens' problem. During their travels, Gilgamesh offends the gods, who respond by killing Enkidu. Enkidu's death causes Gilgamesh to think about his own mortality and prompts him to seek the secret of life. In the process, the king grows in maturity and returns to Uruk in a better position to rule. *See also* Gilgamesh Epic.

Enlil   Enlil is one of the major gods of the Mesopotamian pantheon. Enlil in Sumerian means "lord of the wind" and alludes to the fact that he keeps separate the gods An (heaven) and Ki (earth). Enlil develops into a warlike god and plays a significant role in many ancient myths, including those that describe the creation of the first humans and a devastating flood. In Atrahasis, for instance, Enlil is the one to whom the lesser gods complain about their job digging irrigation ditches, which leads to the creation of the first humans. In Atrahasis as well as Gilgamesh, Enlil is the god who decides to bring the flood to destroy human beings because they are making too much noise. *See also* Atrahasis; Gilgamesh Epic; Sumer.

Enoch, Book of (1 Enoch) Pseudepigraphic work written in the name of the biblical character Enoch, great-grandfather of Noah (Gen. 5:18–29). Also called *The Ethiopic Apocalypse of Enoch*, *1 Enoch* is preserved complete only in ancient Ethiopic (Ge'ez), though fragments survive in Aramaic, Greek, and Latin. It is a composite work representing various periods and writers (300 BC– AD 100). The first part (chaps. 1–36), the Book of Watchers, describes Enoch's journeys to the heavens and includes an account of the fall of the Watchers, angels who fathered the Nephilim (Gen. 6). Most disputed is the central section, known as the Similitudes, or the Parables of Enoch (chaps. 37–71), which refers to an exalted messianic figure known as the Son of Man (a title drawn from Dan. 7). If this section is pre-Christian, it would indicate Jewish use of this title for the Messiah before the time of Christ. *First Enoch* 1:9 is quoted in the book of Jude (v. 14), indicating that the book was known and used by early Christians. It is unclear, however, how much canonical authority was given to it. *See also* Pseudepigrapha, the.

Enuma Elish Name (meaning "When on high … ") given to a Babylonian composition that concerns the elevation of Marduk to head of the pantheon and the construction of his temple (Esagila). Scholars debate whether Enuma Elish was composed during the reign of Hammurabi (eighteenth century BC) or Nebuchadnezzar I (twelfth century BC), two times when the city of Babylon (and thus its chief god Marduk) achieved dominance in Mesopotamia. Enuma Elish generates interest among biblical scholars today because after

Marduk defeats the sea monster Tiamat, he uses her body to create the heavens and the earth and then creates humanity from the clay of the earth and the blood of her demonic consort Qingu. These parallels generate discussion of the similarities and differences with various biblical conceptions of creation (Gen. 1–2; Job 38; Prov. 8; etc). *See also* Akkadian; Babylon; Marduk; Qingu (Kingu); Tiamat.

Ephraim The name of the younger son of Joseph, whom Jacob, his grandfather, blesses as if he is the firstborn. Ephraim's descendants become the strongest tribe in the north, rivaling Judah in the south. After Israel divides in two after the reign of Solomon, the northern tribes as a whole are sometimes called Ephraim.

epic The term derives from Greek and designates a literary type similar in form and content to the *Iliad* and the *Odyssey* by Homer, namely poems that extol deeds of great people (epic legends) or the gods (epic myths). In the ancient Near East, the former would include Enmerkar and the Lord of Aratta and various stories about King Gilgamesh in Sumerian, Atrahasis and Gilgamesh in Akkadian, and Keret and Aqhat in Ugaritic, and the latter would include Inanna and Enki in Sumerian, Enuma Elish in Akkadian, and the Baal Myth in Ugaritic. *See also* Atrahasis; Baal texts; Gilgamesh Epic; Ugaritic.

Epicurean Follower of Epicurus, a Greek philosopher who lived from about 341 to 270 BC. He was a materialist who believed that nothing existed except matter and space. The greatest good in life was therefore the pursuit of pleasure and self-fulfillment. Pleasure for Epicurus was not hedonism but rather the pursuit of positive virtues, such as living modestly, limiting one's desires, and gaining knowledge of the world. As a materialist Epicurus was a critic of religion and superstitious belief. Paul encounters Epicurean philosophers in Athens in Acts 17:18.

epiphany From the Greek *epiphaneia*, meaning "manifestation" or "appearance," and referring to the appearance of God to human beings. In discussions of the OT the term can refer to God's appearance to individuals, such as Abraham (Gen. 17) and Moses (Exod. 3). In the study of the NT, it often refers to a revelation of God's glory through Jesus, such as at the transfiguration (Mark 9:2–3 par.) or when Jesus walks on water (Mark 6:47–52 par.). The Christian feast of Epiphany (January 6) celebrates the incarnation of the Son of God, with a focus on the visit of the Magi (Matt. 2). The Greek term is used five times in the Pastoral Epistles (only once elsewhere in the NT: 2 Thess. 2:8); four of these refer to the second coming (1 Tim. 6:14; 2 Tim. 4:1, 8; Titus 2:13), and one to the incarnation (2 Tim. 1:10). *See also* Christophany; theophany.

Erasmus, Desiderius (1466–1536) Renaissance scholar, theologian, humanist, and Roman Catholic priest. Erasmus was one of the most brilliant minds of his age. Although critical of the abuses of the Roman Catholic Church and sympathetic to many of the concerns of the Protestant Reformers, Erasmus never joined the Reformation and remained loyal to the pope and the Catholic Church. He is best known in biblical studies for his production of the first published Greek NT, a text that became the standard for the Greek text for centuries. Not until the introduction of modern methods of textual criticism following the work of Westcott and Hort did the so-called critical text replace the Textus Receptus, which was based on Erasmus's Greek NT, as the standard Greek text. *See also* critical text; textual criticism; Textus Receptus; Westcott, Brooke Foss.

Esarhaddon The king of Assyria from 680 to 669 BC. He became king after the death of his father, Sennacherib, who had invaded Judah and threatened Jerusalem (2 Kings 19:37 // Isa. 37:38). The book of Ezra (4:2) mentions that Esarhaddon brought foreigners in to live in Palestine. When he died, his son Ashurbanipal took the throne. *See also* Assyria.

eschatology In the narrow sense the term refers to the study of the last days, and in the broad sense, to the study of the future. Prophetic and apocalyptic books of the OT demonstrate eschatological thinking in both the narrow and broad senses. Other texts, such as kingship psalms that celebrated the divinely instituted monarch (Pss. 2; 110; etc.), also have an eschatological sense, anticipating the coming of the future Messiah. NT passages that anticipate future events, particularly the return of Christ at the end of time, are eschatological. At the same time, from the perspective of NT theology, the "last days" are both *already* and *not yet*. They have been inaugurated with the life, death, resurrection, and ascension of Jesus (Acts 2:17; 1 Cor. 10:11; 2 Cor. 5:17) but will be consummated at his second coming. *See also* apocalypticism, apocalyptic literature; Cullmann, Oscar; Dodd, Charles Harold; Ladd, George Eldon.

Essenes A Jewish sect, mentioned by Josephus and other writers (notably Philo), that arose in Israel during the Second Temple period. According to Josephus, while some Essenes married and lived in the towns and villages of Israel, others lived in monastic settlements. He estimates their number at about four thousand. The Essenes were known for their piety, communal sharing of goods, and strict adherence to the law of Moses. Most scholars believe that the Dead Sea Scrolls were produced by an Essene community at Khirbet Qumran. *See also* Dead Sea Scrolls; Josephus.

etiology A story or a part of a story whose purpose is to provide a cause or give an origin for some contemporary phenomenon. A number of biblical stories clearly have an explicit etiological function. Why was Eve named a "woman" (*'ishsha*)? Because she was taken from a man (*'ish*). Historical-critical scholars, particularly of the previous generation, often invoked etiology to explain the original purpose of some OT stories, as if it were the main purpose of the stories. An example is the story of the walking serpent in Genesis 3, whose role in tempting Adam and Eve leads God to punish it by saying it must slither on the ground. *See also* historical criticism.

etymology The study of the origin and history of words and the ways their meanings have changed over time. Etymology can be especially helpful in studying rare words in languages that have a relatively small body of literature, such as classical Hebrew. Tracing the etymology of cognate words in other Semitic languages can give us clues as to the meaning of the related words in Hebrew. On the other hand, etymology can be misleading, since the meaning of a word can change over time, often in unpredictable ways. The history of a word does not necessarily determine its contemporary meaning. For example, the word "pitiful" originally meant "full of pity"—that is, compassionate—but this etymology would be misleading today. James Barr, in particular, sought to draw attention to the inappropriate use of etymology in the study of the biblical languages. *See also* Barr, James.

Eucharist Also known as the Lord's Supper and Communion, the celebration of the ritual meal instituted by Jesus at the Last Supper before his crucifixion (Mark 14:23–24 // Matt. 26:26–29 // Luke 22:15–20 // 1 Cor. 11:23–26). Eucharist means "thanksgiving."

Euphrates The southernmost of the two rivers that run through Mesopotamia (modern Iraq) from Armenia into the Persian Gulf. It is first mentioned in the Bible as one of the four rivers that flow out of Eden (Gen. 2:14) and is mentioned many other times as a prominent river that separates Mesopotamia from the Levant. *See also* Mesopotamia.

Eusebius of Caesarea (ca. 260–340) Bishop of Caesarea Maritima and early church historian, known as "the father of church history." Though a prolific author and scholar, Eusebius is best known for his ten-volume *Ecclesiastical History*, which draws from a wide range of sources to provide a history of the church from its beginning to the time of Constantine.

evolutionary creationism / theistic evolution Evolutionary creationism and theistic evolution are used interchangeably, the former name being preferred by its present advocates because it better communicates the idea that God is the creator. Advocates argue that, while the Bible makes it clear that God created everything, the highly figurative description of the creation in Genesis 1–2 and elsewhere indicates that the Bible does not claim to tell the reader how he created everything. Since the Bible is silent on the mode of creation, it is argued, we should study nature (God's other book) to answer questions of process, and such study leads to the conclusion that God used evolution to create humanity.

exegesis Refers to the act of interpreting and explaining a text. Exegesis seeks to bring out the author's original meaning or the message of the text. Its opposite is eisegesis, which is typically used as a pejorative term referring to reading meaning into the text. *See also* eisegesis.

exile *See* Babylonian exile.

existentialist interpretation Philosophical perspective that views personal and subjective experience as the most fundamental feature of human reality. Existentialists consider individuals to be free and responsible agents who determine their own course in life through personal acts of will. The "father" of Christian existentialism was Søren Kierkegaard (1813–55), who argued that personal experience of God superseded social structures, moral norms, community values, and theological tenets. Perhaps the most well known of existentialist theologians was Paul Tillich (1886–1965), and of biblical scholars, Rudolf Bultmann (1884–1976). Bultmann adopted some of the language of existentialist philosopher Martin Heidegger, asserting that the goal of the gospel was to live a life of "authentic existence" before humanity and God. *See also* Bultmann, Rudolf Karl.

exodus, the From a Greek word that means "departure." When used in biblical studies, the word refers to the account of God's rescue of enslaved Israelites from Egypt allowing them to depart from that oppressive country and begin their journey to the promised land (see Exod. 1–18). The date of the exodus is disputed. The key text in this regard is 1 Kings 6:1, which states that Solomon began to build the temple in the fourth year of his reign, which took place

480 years after the exodus. Since the fourth year of Solomon is dated to around 966 BC, this seems to point to a fifteenth-century-BC exodus. However, the archaeology of sites associated with the store cities in Egypt built while Israel was in captivity (Exod. 1:11) as well as sites associated with the conquest that follows forty years later (particularly Jericho and Ai) does not comport well with that date. Thus some believe 480 is a symbolic number representing twelve generations, since, the argument goes, forty is the symbolic number of a generation. However, since twenty-five years is a more typical time for a generation, twelve generations would last more like three hundred years, and thus 1 Kings 6:1 points to a thirteenth-century-BC event. *See also* conquest, the.

F

farewell discourse As a genre, a farewell discourse is a last address given by a patriarch or leader to his children or followers. It can include recollections, prophecies, and exhortations. Biblical examples include Jacob's testament to his twelve sons (Gen. 49), Moses's final song and blessing to the people of Israel (Deut. 32–33), and Paul's farewell discourse to the elders of Ephesus (Acts 20:17–38). The term is applied especially to Jesus's message delivered to his disciples following the Last Supper in John 13–17. The account follows the evening meal and includes Jesus's washing of the disciples' feet, his predictions of betrayal by Judas and denial by Simon Peter, teaching on himself as the one true way to God, his promise to send the Holy Spirit as his empowering presence, identification of himself as the vine and the disciples as branches, and warnings against the evil world system. The discourse concludes with Jesus's prayer for his disciples (chap. 17). See also *Testaments of the Twelve Patriarchs*.

feminist interpretation Approach to biblical interpretation that examines the biblical text from a feminist perspective, especially with reference to the historical oppression and subjugation of women. This movement found its voice in biblical studies especially in the second half of the twentieth century. Some important feminist biblical scholars include Phyllis Bird, Elisabeth Schüssler Fiorenza, and Phyllis Trible. Prominent feminist theologians include

Rosemary Radford Ruether and Letty Russell. *See also* womanist interpretation.

Fertile Crescent The region that stretches from the Nile Valley in Egypt up through the eastern coast of the Mediterranean and into Syria (the Levant) and then down the Tigris and Euphrates and the alluvial plain that stretches between them to the Persian Gulf. This territory forms a crescent and contains land that can produce crops, especially as compared to the arid lands around them. This area also witnessed the rise of early human civilization, particularly in Egypt and in southern Mesopotamia.

fertility cult Fertility, whether human or agricultural, was a subject of major concern to those who lived in the ancient Near East. While there were zones that could produce crops (Fertile Crescent), many areas were marginal when it came to the necessary rainfall. Thus, some religions of the ancient Near East focused on fertility and had rituals that intended to encourage the birth of children and the growing of crops. The status of fertility religions and rituals in the ancient Near East is debated, with some arguing that the worship of Baal, for instance, was fundamentally a seasonal-cycle religion (with Baal dying during the winter and revivifying in the spring) accompanied by various sexual rituals. Biblical texts may allude to fertility rites, though this too is debated. In Genesis 38, Judah sleeps with his daughter-in-law Tamar, thinking that she is a "shrine prostitute" (vv. 21–22). Some argue that Gomer, Hosea's promiscuous wife, was a shrine prostitute, though there is nothing in the text that explicitly makes that connection. *See also* Baal texts; Fertile Crescent.

Festschrift A book honoring a scholar, generally made up of a collection of essays by colleagues and leaders in the scholar's field of study. The term is German, meaning "celebratory writing." Festschrifen (pl.) are generally produced to celebrate a particular milestone, such as a seventieth birthday or retirement from a distinguished career.

Finkelstein, Israel (1949–) Professor of archaeology at the University of Tel Aviv and codirector of the excavations of the important site of Megiddo. He believes that archaeological remains do not confirm that Jerusalem during the period of David and Solomon was the center of a robust monarchy but rather shows that it was a modest village with a small palace and holy place at best. He is not a full-blown minimalist, but he does argue that the early history of Israel is not reliably told in the Bible and that most of the Bible was written between the seventh and fifth centuries BC. *See also* archaeology; internal transformation model; minimalism.

form criticism (*Formgeschichte*) Field of biblical studies that examines the oral traditions that lie behind a document's written sources. A "form" is a mini genre, such as a lament psalm, a judgment oracle, a parable, or a miracle story. The goals of form criticism are to identify the original *Sitz im Leben* ("setting in life") of the forms and trace their development and transmission history in the community of faith. Old Testament form criticism was pioneered by scholars such as Hermann Gunkel, Martin Noth, and Gerhard von Rad. Pioneers of NT form criticism, which focuses especially on the forms behind the Gospel tradition, include Rudolf Bultmann, Martin Dibelius, and Vincent Taylor. The heyday of form criticism was in the middle of the twentieth century. Interest has waned in recent years because of greater skepticism concerning the ability to identify the original forms and transmission history of oral traditions and because of greater interest in the final form of the biblical documents as works of literature. *See also* Bultmann, Rudolf Karl; Gunkel, Hermann; historical criticism; Noth, Martin; von Rad, Gerhard.

formal equivalent translation No English (or any other modern language) translation of the Bible can be strictly word-for-word and follow the syntax of the original languages and still be understandable. But a formal equivalent, as opposed to a functional equivalent, translation tends toward reflecting the original, sometimes at the expense of readability. Perhaps the clearest example of a formal equivalent translation is an interlinear Bible, where the English translation is placed immediately below the Hebrew, Aramaic, or Greek original. But these are typically used as study helps for beginning language students. The New American Standard Bible (NASB) and the English Standard Version (ESV) are examples of translations that tend toward formal equivalence. *See also* English Standard Version (ESV); functional equivalent translation; New American Standard Bible (NASB).

Formgeschichte *See* form criticism (*Formgeschichte*).

four-source theory *See* Synoptic problem.

framework hypothesis Hypothesis based on the observation that the first three days of creation in Genesis 1 refer to the creation of realms ("forming") and that the second three days refer to the inhabitants of those realms ("filling").

Day 1	Day 2	Day 3
light and darkness	sky and sea	land
Day 4	Day 5	Day 6
sun, moon, and stars	birds and fish	animals and humans

The parallelism between the first three and the second three days suggests that the days are not giving the actual sequence of creation.

functional equivalent translation As opposed to formal equivalent translations, functional equivalent translations are not interested in staying close to the word order or always using the same English rendering for the same Hebrew, Aramaic, or Greek word. Sometimes colloquially referred to as thought-for-thought translation, this approach recognizes that words find their specific meaning in the context of a sentence and even in the broader context of a discourse. The goal of the translator is to engender in the mind of the modern reader the same thought that came to the original readers. Translations that adopt a functional equivalent translation method include the New Living Translation (NLT) and *The Message*. Sometimes functional equivalence is called dynamic equivalence. *See also* formal equivalent translation; *Message, The*; New Living Translation (NLT).

G

Gath An inland city, south of Ekron but still in the northern region of Philistine territory. The people of Ashdod sent the captured ark of the covenant to Gath after God brought disease and devastation on their city. When the same happened in Gath, they sent it to Ekron (1 Sam. 5). Gath may be best known as the city from which Goliath, the Philistine mercenary whom David defeated, came (1 Sam. 17:4). Later, though, David fled to Gath to escape Saul, who wanted to murder him (1 Sam. 21:10–22:1; 27:1–30:31). *See also* Ashdod; Ashkelon; Ekron; Gaza; Philistia.

Gaza The southernmost of the five principal cities of the Philistines. Samson visited a prostitute in Gaza. While he was there, the Philistines tried to kill him, but he escaped by tearing down the city gate and using it as a shield (Judg. 16:1–3). *See also* Ashdod; Ashkelon; Ekron; Gath; Philistia.

gehenna From a Greek transliteration (*geenna*) of the Hebrew phrase *gê [ben] hinnōm*, meaning the "valley of [the son of] Hinnom" (Josh. 15:8; 18:16; Neh. 11:30). The valley is on the south side of Jerusalem and was sometimes used during the period of the monarchy for the horrific practice of sacrificing sons and daughters to the Canaanite gods Baal and Molech (2 Chron. 28:3; 33:6; Jer. 7:31; 19:5–6; 32:35). King Josiah of Judah put an end to the practice by defiling the place (2 Kings 23:10), and it became a garbage dump. Because of its terrible past and the nauseating burning of garbage, during the Second Temple period the name came to be associated with hell, a place of judgment and torment. The Greek word occurs twelve times in the NT and is usually translated "hell" (Matt. 5:22, 29, 30; 10:28; 18:9; 23:15, 33; Mark 9:43, 45, 47; Luke 12:5; James 3:6). Other words for the place of judgment and torment in the NT are *hadēs* (10x), which can sometimes mean simply "death"; *tartarus* (2 Pet. 2:4); and the "lake of fire" (Rev. 20:14). *See also* hades; Sheol.

Gemara *See* rabbinic literature.

General Epistles *See* Catholic (or General) Epistles.

Geneva Bible *See* King James Version (KJV).

genizah A storage area for aging manuscripts. The most famous genizah is the Cairo Genizah located in the synagogue in Cairo and discovered in the 1870s. It contained Jewish manuscripts written in Hebrew, Arabic, and Aramaic on paper and papyrus that date from AD 870 to the nineteenth century. These include biblical, religious, and secular texts. *See also* Damascus Document.

genre A technical term for a literary form or category of composition, such as a poem, a narrative, a proverb, or a letter. Different genres have different communicative functions and so require specific methods of interpretation.

Geschichte, Historie The German term *Geschichte* ("interpreted history") is sometimes contrasted with *Historie* ("the events themselves"). *Geschichte* is understanding events in terms of God's ongoing actions within history. See also *Heilsgeschichte*.

Gezer Calendar Discovered in 1908 at the site of Gezer to the west of Jerusalem, the Gezer Calendar is one of the earliest examples of indigenous writing in ancient Palestine, dating to the tenth century BC. The language is not specifically Hebrew but a related language, perhaps a southern Canaanite dialect. The contents give a calendar of agricultural activities through the year.

Gilgamesh Epic Epic story featuring King Gilgamesh of the Sumerian city of Uruk, who was a real king whose story was aggrandized in the years following his reign (twenty-fifth century BC). Within two hundred years there was already a cycle of stories written in Sumerian about this king. Biblical scholars are particularly interested in the Old Babylonian and neo-Assyrian version of the story about Gilgamesh because of certain biblical parallels, most notably the account of the flood. At the beginning of the story, Gilgamesh is a young, immature king of a city whose citizens appeal to the gods to help them against his thoughtless abuses. The gods respond by creating Enkidu, a primeval man, who is lured into the city by a prostitute. He fights Gilgamesh but loses. Still the people's prayers are answered when Gilgamesh and Enkidu strike up a friendship and go out on adventures together. During their journeys, Gilgamesh insults the goddess Inanna, who complains to her father, who responds by killing Enkidu. As Enkidu dies in the arms of Gilgamesh, the king realizes that he too is mortal, and so he sets out in search of life. This search brings him to Utnapishtim, the only human being who has been granted eternal life. Gilgamesh asks him how he achieved such an enviable status, and this question leads Utnapishtim to tell him the story of the flood. The account bears close similarity to the biblical account found in Genesis 6–9 and has engendered different theories about their relationship. In any case, by relating the story of the flood, Utnapishtim is telling Gilgamesh that the king cannot find eternal life in that way. At the end of the epic, Gilgamesh returns home, and as he sees the walls of Uruk, he realizes that his lasting fame will come about if he is a good king to that city. *See also* Akkadian; Enlil; Sumer.

gloss A term that carries various senses in biblical studies. In textual criticism a gloss is a marginal or in-text note added by a scribe to a manuscript. The gloss often clarifies or explains the meaning of the text. In translational studies, a gloss refers to the rendering of a word or lexeme in a particular context. The term is commonly used to avoid the exact identification of a word in one language with a word in another. For example, it is not correct to say that the Greek word *sarx* means "flesh," since flesh is only one possible sense within the Greek term's large semantic range. "Flesh" is instead a gloss used to roughly approximate the sense of *sarx* in a particular context. *See also* textual criticism.

glossolalia Greek term meaning "speaking in tongues," or "speaking in other languages." As one of the so-called sign gifts, speaking in tongues appears prominently in the book of Acts (2:3–4, 11; 10:46; 19:6) and Paul's first letter to the Corinthians (chaps. 12–14). While tongues in Acts 2 appear to be human languages, elsewhere the phenomenon resembles an ecstatic prayer language. Speaking in tongues sometimes accompanies an individual's initial reception of the Holy Spirit (10:45–46; 19:6). In 1 Corinthians, Paul calls on the church to practice tongues in an orderly and disciplined manner, which builds up the church rather than causing disorder and conflict. The gift of tongues has been controversial in the history of the church, especially with the modern growth of Pentecostalism and the charismatic movement.

gnosticism, *gnōsis* Gnosticism is the designation given to a variety of religious movements arising in the late first and early second centuries that shared the same general worldview and certain core beliefs. The gnostic belief system arose from the philosophical foundation of Platonism, a dualistic perspective that contrasted the pure spiritual realm and the material world. The gnostic foundation myth concerned the supreme god, or *plērōma* (meaning "fullness"), who was wholly transcendent and pure spirit. Emanating from this god were many *aeons*, or lesser spirit beings. One of these (sometimes called the demiurge), created the fallen material world. In contrast to Judaism and Christianity, where God's physical creation is good and human beings bear the image of God, gnosticism saw the material world as evil and the physical body as something to escape. Gnostics taught that a person gained salvation through secret "knowledge" (*gnōsis*) of their true spiritual identity and heavenly origin. Salvation is not a gift from God on the basis of Christ's death on the cross, as Christianity teaches, but is the discovery within oneself of this true spiritual identity. The goal of gnosticism is to return to the realm of pure spirit.

Jesus Christ became in gnosticism one aeon or emanation, sent to teach humans about their true spiritual nature. Gnostics rejected the incarnation of Christ (that God became a human being) and the saving significance of his death on the cross. Salvation does not come through sacrifice and atonement but through *gnōsis*, secret knowledge. Gnosticism became a major rival to Christianity in the second and third centuries. The most influential gnostics were the Valentinians, whose beliefs arose from the teachings of Valentinus (ca. 100–153), a prominent second-century leader in the church at Rome. A number of early church writers labeled the movement heretical and wrote against it, including Justin Martyr (ca. 100–168), Irenaeus (ca. 130–202), Clement of Alexandria (ca. 150–216), Tertullian (ca. 155–230), and Origen (ca. 182–251). Until the twentieth century, most of our knowledge about gnosticism came from these opponents. The Nag Hammadi Codices, discovered in 1945 in Egypt, provide primary-source accounts of their beliefs. *See also* Nag Hammadi Library.

Good News Translation (GNT) The NT of this version, published in 1966, was originally called Today's English Version (TEV) and Good News for Modern Man. The NT was translated by Robert Bratcher in consultation with the American Bible Society. The whole Bible was published in 1976 as the Good News Bible and eventually renamed the Good News Translation (GNT). The TEV was the first English version to consciously adopt the functional (dynamic) equivalent method of translation being developed by Eugene Nida and his colleagues at Wycliffe Bible Translators and the United Bible Societies. *See also* functional equivalent translation.

gospel/Gospel Lowercase "gospel" refers to the message of salvation made available through the life, death, and resurrection of Jesus Christ. For example, the apostle Paul often speaks of the "gospel" he preached (1 Thess. 2:2, 4, 8, 9). The English term translates the Greek *euangelion*, which means "good news." Uppercase "Gospel" refers to a book recounting the story of Jesus of Nazareth. The term is chiefly used of the biblical Gospels—Matthew, Mark, Luke, and John—but is also used of the nonbiblical "apocryphal" gospels (often with a lowercase *g* in reference to noncanonical works).

Gospel of Peter An apocryphal gospel written pseudonymously in Peter's name, probably in the mid-second century AD. The work, only part of which has survived, recounts the story of Jesus from the end of his trial to the resurrection appearances. It appears to be dependent on the canonical Gospels and other sources. It has a strong anti-Jewish and apologetic focus, defending the reality of the resurrection against contrary claims. The author speaks in the first person, eventually identifying himself as Simon Peter, the brother of Andrew (14.60). Various early Christian writers refer to the work, some rejecting its authenticity and treating it as docetic (*see* docetism). The gospel was known to have existed from references to it in the early church fathers, but it was rediscovered in 1886 by the French archaeologist Urbain Bouriant.

Gospel of Thomas An apocryphal gospel written pseudonymously in Thomas's name, probably in the second century AD. A copy of the *Gospel* was discovered in Egypt in 1945 together with other works known as the Nag Hammadi Library, a mostly gnostic collection. The *Gospel* includes 114 sayings of Jesus, some of which have parallels in the Synoptic Gospels and many of which reflect gnostic theology. Though the work was written in Coptic, the ancient language of Egypt, fragments of a Greek text were discovered at Oxyrhynchus, and most scholars believe the *Gospel* was originally written in Greek. The *Gospel* begins, "These are the secret words which the living Jesus spoke, and which Didymus Judas Thomas wrote." Thomas is likely the earliest and is widely considered the most important of the apocryphal gospels. The *Gospel of Thomas* should not be confused with the somewhat-later *Infancy Gospel of*

Thomas, one of the legendary tales of the childhood of Jesus. *See also* gnosticism, *gnōsis;* Nag Hammadi Library.

Gottwald, Norman K. (1926–) American professor of OT who taught for many years at Union Theological Seminary in New York City from a Marxist interpretive perspective. He was an early practitioner of the social-scientific method of study of the OT. He is best known for his advocacy in favor of the revolutionary model of the conquest. *See also* Marxist interpretation; social-scientific interpretation.

Griesbach hypothesis *See* Synoptic problem.

Gunkel, Hermann (1862–1932) One of the most influential shapers of historical-critical methodology in the early twentieth century. Gunkel was a German OT scholar credited particularly with the development of form criticism. He was a leading member of the history of religions school, which was current in this day. His primary work was focused on Genesis and Psalms. *See also* form criticism (*Formgeschichte*); historical criticism; history of religions school (*Religionsgeschichtliche Schule*).

H

hades In Greek mythology, Hades was the brother of Zeus and Poseidon and the god of the underworld, which eventually took on his name. Hades came to be viewed as a gloomy place of darkness where souls went after death. In the NT, the Greek *hadēs* can refer simply to death / the grave or to a place of torment for the wicked following death (Luke 16:23). Some theologians consider hades to be an interim place before the final judgment, at which time death and hades will be cast into the lake of fire (Rev. 20:13). *See also* gehenna; Sheol.

haggadah Hebrew term for Talmudic writings that function as narrative or illustration. It is often contrasted with halakah, which refers to legal material or commandments. The term is more specifically and more commonly used today for the text that sets forth the order of the Passover seder—the (Passover) haggadah.

halakah Hebrew term for the whole body of Jewish law, both written and oral. It is usually said to contain 613 commandments. Though often translated as "Jewish law," "halakah" more specifically refers to a "way of walking," or "way of living." Halakah, which is legal material, is sometimes contrasted with haggadah, which is narrative or illustration.

Hammurabi King of Babylon in the early eighteenth century BC. In the aftermath of the destruction of the neo-Sumerian alliance centered on the city of Ur, Hammurabi led during the rise of the first flourishing of a Semitic empire centered in the city of Babylon and thus established what today is called the Old Babylonian period, which lasted to approximately 1600 BC. Unless Hammurabi is Amraphel, one of the invading Near Eastern kings who plundered Canaan during the time of Abraham (Gen. 14), he is not mentioned in the Bible. However, his law code has been the object of study by biblical scholars, who are interested in studying the ancient Near Eastern background to biblical law. Hammurabi's law code is not the oldest law code that we know from the region, since we have Sumerian examples from the last part of the third millennium BC. Most of the laws have a casuistic form ("If . . . , then . . .") rather than the form of a general ethical principle; thus Hammurabi's code is most similar to biblical case law rather than the Ten Commandments. The Code of Hammurabi covers many of the same general topics (murder, theft, sexual crimes, slavery, marriage) and occasionally even specific topics (laws concerning a goring ox), but this similarity is likely the result of legal traditions rather than borrowing. Interestingly, in the Code of Hammurabi punishments differ on the basis of whether crimes are committed against land-owning citizens (*awilum*), slaves (*ardum*), or a middle category of person (*mushkenum*). *See also* Babylon.

Hammurabi, Code of *See* Hammurabi.

Hanukkah Jewish festival celebrating the victory of the Maccabees over Antiochus IV "Epiphanes" and the Seleucid Empire, and the establishment of Jewish independence (166–63 BC). "Hanukkah" means "dedication" and refers to the rededication of the temple by Judas Maccabeus on Chislev 25, 164 BC, exactly three years after its defilement by Antiochus. The celebration is also called the "Festival of Lights," since the victory represented the triumph of light over darkness. A later legend recounts how an oil lamp in the Jerusalem temple miraculously burned for eight days with only one day's supply of oil. The account of the victory of Judas and his brothers appears in the apocryphal books of 1 and 2 Maccabees. *See also* Maccabees, Maccabean revolt.

hapax legomenon A Greek phrase meaning "once spoken" and referring to Hebrew or Greek words that occur only once in the Bible. The phrase can also be used of words that occur only once in the whole body of Hebrew or Greek literature. A word that is a *hapax legomenon* (or *hapax* for short) can be difficult to translate because of the lack of precedent in earlier literature.

hapiru *See* Amarna tablets.

haplography A term used in textual criticism for a type of scribal error, the inadvertent omission of a letter, word, or phrase because of its repetition. For example, scribes would occasionally leave out a whole line of text if the previous line ended with the same word. Its opposite is dittography ("double writing"), when a scribe inadvertently writes a letter, word, or phrase twice. See also *homoioteleuton*; textual criticism.

harmonization Provides explanations for what appear to be historical contradictions or tensions between biblical texts. For instance, the book of Kings presents King Abijah of Judah as a thoroughly negative figure. Indeed, the text calls him Abijam ("My father is Yam," a reference to the god of the sea, who represents chaos) and names Absalom as his mother's father. In Chronicles, he is called Abijah ("My father is Yahweh") and is a thoroughly positive figure. His mother's father is not Absalom but Uriel of Gibeah. A possible, even likely, harmonization would say that the Kings account selects negative stories about Abijah because it was written during the exile to answer the question of why Judah was judged, while Chronicles chooses positive stories since it is written in the postexilic period and encouraging stories are called for. Associating this king with Absalom, David's rebellious son, and calling him Abijam is a further way of presenting a negative picture, while Chronicles chooses another ancestor, Uriel, who did not have the same negative connotations. There is nothing wrong with harmonizations as long as it is recognized that they are speculative and as long as they do not distract the interpreter from noting the purposes for the individual presentations.

harmony of the Gospels A volume that brings together the four Gospels into a single story to provide a chronological and harmonized account of the life of Jesus. The earliest known harmony is the *Diatessaron*, compiled by Tatian in the second century AD. Harmonies can either provide a single continuous account or place the four Gospels in parallel columns. See also *Diatessaron*.

Harnack, Adolf von (1851–1930) German Lutheran theologian and NT scholar whose classic work *What Is Christianity?* (1901) is often viewed as the epitome of the "liberal Jesus" characteristic of the nineteenth-century quest for the historical Jesus. Harnack argued for the strong influence of hellenization on the early Christian movement and rejected doctrines that he claimed arose in the early church rather than with the historical Jesus. Jesus, he asserted, was a social reformer teaching the fatherhood of God, the brotherhood of humanity, and the eternal value of the human soul. Harnack rejected the historicity of the Gospel of John, attributing its theology to later speculation about the nature of Jesus. *See also* quest for the historical Jesus.

Hasidim From a Hebrew word meaning "holy ones" and adopted by those Jews who opposed the adoption of Hellenistic and pagan traditions during the period of Greek domination over Israel (334–164 BC). Their opponents, the Hellenists, encouraged the adoption of Greek language, culture, and religion. It was this struggle between the Hasidim and the Hellenists that provoked the Maccabean revolt. Despite the victory of the Maccabees, this struggle between traditionalists and progressives continued throughout the Greco-Roman period. *See also* Hellenism, Hellenistic; Maccabees, Maccabean revolt.

Hasmoneans Name given to the dynasty of Jewish kings that rose to the throne of Israel during the Maccabean revolt and ruled for the next century. The term is a family name taken from Hasmon, likely the father or grandfather of Mattathias, the Jewish priest who launched the Maccabean revolt. The dynasty may be dated 135–37

BC, from the reign of Simon, son of Mattathias and brother of Judas Maccabeus, to the establishment of the Herodian dynasty under Herod the Great by the Romans. *See also* Maccabees, Maccabean revolt.

Hatti An Indo-European nation-state that flourished in central-east Anatolia (modern Turkey) and northern Syria from about 1800 to 1200 BC, when it was brought to an end by an invasion of the Sea Peoples. At its height, Hatti vied with Egypt and Mesopotamian powers in the region. The literature of Hatti includes a number of different genres; perhaps the most important for biblical studies are their international treaties written in Akkadian, the lingua franca of the day. These treaties, particularly the vassal treaties between the Hatti and a lesser country, have been compared to biblical covenant texts in form and concept, particularly the book of Deuteronomy. The inhabitants of Hatti are commonly referred to as Hittites.

Haustafeln *See* household codes (*Haustafeln*).

Hebrew language Most of the OT is written in Hebrew (notable exceptions include Ezra 4:8–6:18; 7:12–16; Dan. 2:4–7:28, all written in Aramaic). Hebrew is a Northwest Semitic language most closely related to Eblaite, Ugaritic, Aramaic, and other, less attested languages, as well as Eastern Semitic languages like Akkadian and Southern Semitic languages like Arabic. Hebrew is an alphabetic language that has twenty-two letters, all consonants. During the Middle Ages, the Masoretes added vowels to the biblical text by developing a system of points that were added above and below consonants. The earliest surviving written Hebrew we have comes from around the tenth century BC, though it was likely the language spoken in Israel beginning around 1200 BC. While Hebrew continued to be understood and written among scholars, it ceased to be a spoken language sometime after the destruction of Jerusalem, being replaced by Aramaic. Modern Hebrew was created in the nineteenth century AD as part of the modern Zionist movement using the approximately nine thousand words from the Bible as a base and supplementing them with tens of thousands of other words and creating a different verbal system. *See also* Akkadian; Arabic; Aram, Aramaic; Eblaite; Northwest Semitic; Ugaritic.

Heilsgeschichte German term often translated "salvation history," "redemptive history," or "sacred history." The term refers to a theological interpretation that views the biblical text as an account of God's redemptive or saving actions within history. It was popularized especially in the 1950s and '60s by Gerhard von Rad in the study of the OT with reference to the theological perspective found in Deuteronomy and the Hexateuch. Oscar Cullmann utilized the term in interpreting the NT to contrast a theological reading of Scripture with Rudolf Bultmann's existentialist approach. The term is commonly used today of Luke's overall plan in Luke-Acts to place the coming of Jesus and the establishment of the early church in the larger framework of God's dealings with Israel and his redemptive purposes within history. *See also* Bultmann, Rudolf Karl; Cullmann, Oscar; *Geschichte, Historie*; von Rad, Gerhard.

Hellenism, Hellenistic From the Greek word *Hellas*, meaning Greece, Hellenism refers to the adoption of Greek culture and language. The term arose with the conquests of Alexander the Great of the Eastern Mediterranean in the fourth century BC (356–353 BC). Alexander viewed Greek culture as true civilization, superior to all others, and encouraged its adoption following his conquests. *See also* Hasidim.

hendiadys Hendiadys refers to two (or more) words that are either placed next to each other or connected by a copula but that refer to one idea. The existence of hendiadys can be disputed, but many scholars will suggest examples. For instance, it can be debated whether the frequently appearing word pair *sedeqa umishpat* should be translated "righteousness and justice" or "social justice." The latter would be an example of treating the pair as a hendiadys.

A NT example might be John 14:6, where Jesus's assertion that he is "the way, the truth, and the life" could mean "the one true way to life."

Hengel, Martin (1926–2009) German NT scholar and historian of early Judaism. Hengel specialized in the origins of Christianity. As longtime professor of NT and early Judaism at the University of Tübingen, Hengel did much to demonstrate the relationship of Judaism and Hellenism and confirmed against the history of religions school the Jewish background to early Christianity (see *Judaism and Hellenism: Studies in Their Encounter in Palestine during the Early Hellenistic Period* [2 vols.; 1974]). His wide-ranging research into Christian origins did much to undermine the Bultmannian skepticism that had dominated so much of German NT scholarship. *See also* Bultmann, Rudolf Karl; history of religions school (*Religionsgeschichtliche Schule*).

herem A Hebrew term that is difficult to translate. It is a noun that comes from the verb *haram*, which means "to completely annihilate" and is often used in contexts of warfare within the promised land where God calls on his people to completely destroy the previous inhabitants of the land (e.g., Deut. 7:2). This type of warfare is sometimes referred to in the literature as *herem* warfare, as opposed to warfare outside the promised land, where prisoners of war may be taken (see Deut. 20). In *herem* warfare, not only must all the enemy be killed but none of the plunder should be taken for individual gain; it must either be destroyed or turned over to the Lord (see Josh. 7 and 1 Kings 15 for violations).

hermeneutics The science of biblical interpretation, which includes the development of a theory of meaning, principles of exegesis, and methods related to discerning the contemporary significance of the text. *See also* exegesis.

Hermetic literature A collection of Egyptian wisdom texts written in Greek and usually dated to the second and third centuries AD. Most recount the teaching of Hermes Trismegistus ("Hermes

Three-Times-Great"), Egyptian god of wisdom, and include ad-dresses to his disciples. The texts deal with an array of topics, in-cluding philosophy, theology, astrology, nature, magic, and even alchemy. The Hermetic literature is likely the work of various authors but takes a generally consistent theological perspective. These works have philosophical connections to Neoplatonism and gnosticism, focusing on the oneness of God and defending pagan religious practices. *See also* gnosticism, *gnōsis*.

Hexapla A massive edition of the Bible composed of six versions, originally compiled by the early church father Origen (AD 185–254). The *Hexapla* included (1) the Hebrew text, (2) the Secunda (Hebrew transliterated into Greek letters), and four Greek versions: (3) Aquila of Sinope, (4) Symmachus the Ebionite, (5) Theodo-tion, and (6) an eclectic recension (an edition derived from various sources) of the Septuagint. The full text originally existed in sixteen volumes and was over five thousand pages long. Only fragments have survived. *See also* Aquila of Sinope; Origen; recension; Sep-tuagint; Symmachus; Theodotion.

Hexateuch Hexateuch means "six scrolls" and refers to the theory held by some scholars (like Gerhard von Rad) that the sources of the Pentateuch continue into the book of Joshua, thus forming a six-part (rather than five-part) book. *See also* Pentateuch; von Rad, Gerhard.

hieroglyphics The earliest form of Egyptian writing, developed sometime around 3000 BC. The term means "sacred engravings." Each symbol—and there are about one thousand—represents either a morpheme (a carrier of meaning) or a sound. Hieroglyphic Egyptian uses determinatives; a determinative is a symbol that identifies the type of word that follows it. Hieroglyphic Egyptian was deciphered in the early nineteenth century after the discovery of the Rosetta Stone, which contained three columns of writing, one in hieroglyphics, one in demotic (a later form of Egyptian writing), and one in Greek. *See also* Egypt.

high places   "High places" (Heb. *bamot*) refers to local shrines that were set up in the hill country of Israel and Judah. These shrines were forbidden (whether dedicated to false gods or even to Yahweh) after the construction of the central sanctuary (temple) by the law of centralization (Deut. 12). The book of Kings identifies the construction of high places (only suppressed by a few kings [most notably Hezekiah and Josiah]) as one reason why God sent Israel into exile.

Hillel   Famous rabbi of the Second Temple period (lived ca. 110 BC–AD 10) who was influential in the development of the traditions behind the Mishnah, the written code of Jewish law. Hillel was born in Babylon but came to Jerusalem at about age forty and lived there the rest of his life. The school of Hillel (meaning the disciples who gathered around him and the body of teaching he promoted) was more liberal in its interpretation of Torah than its chief rival, the school of Shammai. For example, while the school of Shammai limited the grounds for divorce to adultery, Hillel said a man could divorce his wife for almost any reason (*m. Gittin* 9.10). Hillel is also well known for explicating the negative version of the Golden Rule: "What is hateful to you, do not do to anyone else; that is the whole Law, all else is commentary" (*b. Shabb.* 31a). *See also* rabbinic literature; Shammai.

historical criticism   Term applied to a variety of methods that were developed in the Western world to analyze the biblical text in the centuries following the Enlightenment and the development of the scientific method (seventeenth to twentieth centuries). Among the methods of historical criticism are form criticism, source criticism, redaction criticism, tradition criticism, and canonical criticism. Historical criticism seeks to determine through "objective" methodologies the historical processes by which the biblical text came to be. Historical criticism is sometimes called "higher criticism," distinguishing it from "lower criticism," or textual criticism. *See also* canonical criticism/approach; form criticism (*Formgeschichte*); redaction criticism (*Redaktionsgeschichte*); source criticism; textual criticism; tradition-historical criticism.

historical-grammatical interpretation Method of biblical interpretation (hermeneutics) that seeks to discover the biblical author's intended meaning within its historical and literary context. The method tends to be practiced by conservative biblical scholars and to assume a high view of the authority and inspiration of the Bible. It was labeled historical-grammatical especially in opposition to the historical-critical methodologies, which tend toward a more skeptical, rationalistic, and antisupernatural view of Scripture. The method also stands against allegorical or spiritualizing interpretations of Scripture. *See also* hermeneutics; historical criticism.

Historie See *Geschichte, Historie*.

historiography The term can be used of the writing of history in general or to the academic study of how history is written. In this sense it refers not to the events themselves but to how they are depicted. In biblical studies the term is perhaps most commonly used with reference to Luke-Acts. Luke writes a selective history to demonstrate that the events surrounding Jesus of Nazareth and the rise of the Christian movement were the work of God and that the church of his day represents the true people of God in the present age.

history of interpretation The history of interpretation examines how a biblical book or passage has been interpreted through history going back to the earliest interpretations that are still extant. During much of the twentieth century, this subject was ignored, particularly by those who practiced historical-critical and historical-grammatical interpretation, feeling that premodern interpretations were of little value to discovering the original intention of the biblical authors. Today, there has been a resurgence of appreciation for these earlier studies as throwing light on the meaning of the biblical books and as a corrective to a more atomistic approach to interpretation. *See also* historical criticism; historical-grammatical interpretation.

history of religions school (*Religionsgeschichtliche Schule*) In the field of biblical studies, this school of thought developed primarily in Germany at the University of Göttingen under the leadership of OT and NT professors, including Gunkel, Duhm, Wrede, Bousset, and Troeltsch. Their influence began in the last decade of the nineteenth and into the early twentieth century. Originally, they were reacting against the liberal theology of Albrecht Ritschl, arguing that he and other scholars like him did not take seriously the religious context of the biblical texts. Thus, the Göttingen school looked at the NT in the context of Greco-Roman religion and Judaism while the OT was studied in the context of ancient Near Eastern religions. *See also* Bousset, Wilhelm; Gunkel, Hermann; Wrede, William.

Hittites The term "Hittite" is sometimes used to refer to certain pre-Israelite inhabitants of Canaan (CSB uses "Hethite"). It is also used in reference to the inhabitants of Anatolia (*see* Hatti). The connection between these residents of Canaan and the people of Anatolia is not clear, though it is unlikely that they are ethnically related. Perhaps there was a political relationship at one point.

Holiness Code (H) Refers to the collection of laws found in Leviticus 17–26. The name Holiness Code derives from the statement "I am the LORD your God" (18:2, 4; 19:3–4, 10; 20:7) as the reason why Israel is to obey the law, from the statement "Be holy because I, the LORD your God, am holy" (Lev. 19:2; 20:26), and from the frequent use of the term "holy" throughout. The Holiness Code contains laws about handling blood (chap. 17), about incest, and about other sexual infractions (chaps. 18; 20); laws about sacrifices and priests (chaps. 21–22) and the Jubilee (chap. 25); and other miscellaneous laws. The law is followed by blessings for obedience to the law (26:1–13) and curses for disobedience (26:14–46). Historical critics tend to assign the Holiness Code to the Priestly source (P), though many believe that it was a separate collection of laws that was added to P. *See also* Documentary Hypothesis.

Holman Christian Standard Bible *See* Christian Standard Bible (CSB).

holy war A term never found in the Bible, it is used to describe the type of warfare that God requires Israel to wage within the promised land. The term "holy war" is appropriate because God makes his presence known in the battle (often symbolically represented by the presence of the ark of the covenant), thus rendering the battlefield holy. See also *herem.*

homoioteleuton A term used in textual criticism meaning "similar endings." It refers to a type of scribal error, the inadvertent skipping of a letter, word, or line that ends the same as a previous one. *See also* haplography; textual criticism.

Hort, Fenton John Anthony (1828–92) *See* Westcott, Brooke Foss.

hortatory An adjective meaning "with the goal of exhortation or encouragement." The term is often used with reference to biblical passages, especially in the Epistles, where the intention is to encourage readers to a particular course of action. A similar word is "paraenetic," which refers to material of practical application intended to provoke the reader to response. *See also* paraenesis.

house of David inscription A memorial inscription by an unnamed king—though some believe he is Hazael of Damascus—written in Aramaic. For biblical studies, this inscription is important for mentioning "the house of David." Discovered at Tell Dan in 1993–94, this inscription is dated to the late ninth century BC and provides solid evidence in favor of a historical David, who ruled in Israel in the previous century.

household codes (*Haustafeln*) A literary form found in various NT epistles, where instructions are given to maintain order and functionality in Christian households. Household codes (called in German *Haustafeln*) have precedent in Greek and Roman ethics and concern relationships between husbands and wives, parents and children, masters and slaves, and citizens and their rulers. Their purpose in the NT is to encourage Christians to live a peaceful and orderly life in the midst of Greco-Roman hierarchical society and patriarchal family structures. The main household codes in the NT are found in Ephesians 5:22–6:9; Colossians 3:18–4:1; 1 Timothy 2:1–15; 6:1–2; Titus 2:1–10; and 1 Peter 2:13–3:7. Because the household codes accept (affirm?) patriarchy and slavery, enormous debate has centered on their applicability for today. Are these God's standards of behavior for Christians of every time and place? Or are they morally relative, reflecting God's cultural condescension to societal values of the Greco-Roman world? The debate often pits complementarians, who claim women should be submissive to their husbands and must not exercise authority over men in the church, with egalitarians, who claim full equality of status and roles for men and women in the church and the home.

Hyksos The name given by native Egyptians to a group of West Semitic people who entered Egypt and by 1700 BC had taken over Lower Egypt, the northern part, and ruled from their capital at Avaris (biblical Zoan). Upper Egypt, the southern part, remained under the rule of a native Egyptian dynasty, which was the one, under the leadership of Kamose and then Ahmoses, that expelled the Hyksos from Egypt around 1570 BC, thus ending the so-called Second Intermediate period and initiating the New Kingdom period. The Hyksos are not mentioned in the Bible, but some speculate that the story of Joseph fits best during the reign of a Hyksos pharaoh and that the Egyptians' experience of the Hyksos may have fed their fear of the Israelites during the period leading up to the exodus. *See also* Egypt.

hyperbole A form of figurative language that intentionally exaggerates to produce an effect or to make a point. Examples include the depiction of the conquest in Joshua 1–12, which describes Joshua as taking all of the land (see summary statement in Josh. 12), when the second half of the book of Joshua and Judges 1 make it clear that the Canaanites still possessed much of the land even after the death of Joshua. Joshua 1–12 focuses on success in order to celebrate the beginning of the fulfillment of the Abrahamic promise of land (Gen. 12:1–3). Hyperbole is also common in Jesus's teaching, for example, when he tells the religious leaders that, with reference to the law, they "strain out a gnat, but gulp down a camel" (Matt. 23:24).

hypotaxis Grammatical subordination of phrases or clauses, as in the subordination of a participial phrase to the main clause of a sentence. While Hebrew grammar tends to favor parataxis, meaning a series of parallel clauses, Greek grammar favors hypotaxis, with a single main clause and a number of subordinate clauses. In the NT, the more Semitic writers tend toward greater use of parataxis (John; Mark; etc.), while writers with higher literary abilities tend toward hypotaxis (Luke; Hebrews; etc.).

I

Ibn Ezra, Abraham (ca. 1089–1167) Famous Jewish biblical scholar, poet, and philosopher of the Middle Ages. Ibn Ezra wrote prolifically on Hebrew grammar and wrote commentaries on almost every book in the Hebrew Bible. In contrast to many of his contemporaries, he focused on the plain or natural sense of the text rather than appealing to rabbinic allegorical or Cabalistic (mystical) interpretations. For this reason, he is often claimed as an advocate for the historical-grammatical method. Yet he also refused to harmonize difficult texts, tended at times toward rationalism, and may have doubted Mosaic authorship of the Pentateuch. For these reasons, he has also been identified by some as a pioneer in historical criticism. *See also* historical criticism; historical-grammatical interpretation.

Ignatius (ca. 35–108) Early Christian writer and bishop of Antioch. Tradition holds that he was a disciple of John the apostle. Ignatius wrote a series of letters to churches dealing with theological and ecclesiological issues on his way to face trial in Rome, where he was martyred around 108. These seven letters, six to churches and one to Polycarp, bishop of Smyrna, now make up part of the collection known as the Apostolic Fathers, the earliest postapostolic writings from the early church. *See also* apostolic fathers.

immigration model In the 1950s two German scholars, Albrecht Alt and his student Martin Noth, argued that archaeological research did not support the idea that Israel occupied Canaan by means of a violent conquest in the early Iron Age. They instead proposed that Israel was a result of a peaceful immigration into the area. This view fails to account for how Israel not only came into the land but also succeeded in deposing the Canaanites. Thus, while notable as the first alternative model of the conquest, other theories such as the revolution model and the internal transformation model are preferred by those who reject the biblical account of conquest or the minimalist denial that there is any historical reference behind the book of Joshua. *See* also Alt, Albrecht; immigration model; internal transformation model; minimalism; Noth, Martin.

implied author A category from the methodology of narrative criticism, which analyzes biblical narratives from the perspective of story. The implied author is the author as discernible from the narrative strategy of the text itself, apart from anything external to that text. This is distinct from the real (historical) author, to whom a modern reader has no direct access. It is also distinct from the narrator, who is the voice we hear telling the story. For example, a narrator may speak in the first person as a fictional character expressing racist views, as in Mark Twain's novel *Huckleberry Finn*—views that differ from both those of the real author and those of the implied author. *See also* implied reader; narrative criticism.

implied reader A category from the methodology of narrative criticism, which analyzes biblical narratives from the perspective of story. The implied reader is the imaginary reader who responds appropriately to the narrative strategy of the text. This is distinct from a real reader, who may misunderstand the story or fail to respond as the author intended. Implied readers can be broken down further into two categories, "informed readers" and "naïve readers." The informed reader already knows where the story is going and so responds accordingly. The naïve reader, or "first-time reader," responds appropriately at any particular point in the progress of the story. For example, a first-time implied reader will be shocked when Jesus announces that the Messiah must suffer and die (Mark 8:31). An informed implied reader, by contrast, already understands that the mission of Jesus includes suffering and death. *See also* implied author; narrative criticism.

imprecations   Imprecations are curses. In biblical studies, the term is typically applied to sections of lament psalms (for example, Ps. 69:22–28) where the sufferer calls on God to punish the enemy and those around him. Some scholars use the term "imprecatory psalm," but there are no psalms that are completely devoted to imprecations, though Psalm 109 comes close. Thus it is better to think of imprecations as part of a lament. Jesus's "woes" against the religious leaders in Matthew 23:13–38 and against the rich and powerful in his sermon in Luke 6:24–26 are also imprecations.

inclusio   Also called "envelope structure" or "envelope figure," "framing," or "bookends," this literary device is the repeating of a phrase, line, theme, or motif at the beginning and end of a section of text. Psalm 8 provides a well-known example since it begins (v. 1) and ends (v. 9) with the statement: "Lord, our Lord, how majestic is your name in all the earth!" (NIV). Like all refrains, the content of the repetition becomes an important idea in the poem, and the location at the beginning and end of the poem creates a sense of opening and closure of the poem or poetic unit. *See also* poetry.

inerrancy of Scripture   A doctrine of biblical authority advocated by many evangelical Protestant thinkers. As the name suggests, it asserts that since the Bible is the Word of God and since God does not lie or mislead, his Word must be without error. A more precise definition of inerrancy is that the Bible in its autographs (the putative but nonextant original copy of the final form of each biblical book) is without error in everything that it intends to teach. *See also* autograph.

infallibility of Scripture   The doctrine of the infallibility of Scripture asserts that Scripture is wholly true in its claims. In some contexts infallibility means essentially the same as inerrancy, without error in everything it asserts. In other contexts, however, the term is used to avoid some of the claims of inerrantists. In these contexts infallibility means that the Bible is completely trustworthy in matters of faith and practice but that it is not necessarily without error in other areas, such as historical accuracy or scientific understanding. *See also* inerrancy of Scripure.

inscription Refers to a relatively short written statement on any medium, including stone, metal, clay pots, tablets, walls, papyrus, and so on.

intelligent design (ID) A movement and school of thought that points to what is called "irreducible complexity" to challenge the idea that evolution provides the explanation of the origin of human beings. Since irreducibly complex structures cannot be explained by evolutionary processes, an intelligent designer is necessary to explain the origin of humanity. Critics point out that such assertions are no more than "God-of-the-gaps arguments" and that what ID advocates suggest are not explained by evolutionary mechanisms will eventually be explained.

intercalation A literary device associated especially with narrative whereby one story is interrupted by another before reaching its conclusion. The two stories frequently relate to the same theme or mutually interpret one another. This is one of Mark's favorite literary devices in his Gospel. For example, the account of Jesus's cursing of the fig tree and its subsequent withering is interrupted by his clearing of the Jerusalem temple (Mark 11:12–21). Both incidents symbolically relate to the failure of Israel's leaders and the resulting judgment that will overtake the nation.

internal transformation model Scholars who doubt the historical reliability of the biblical account of the conquest of Canaan must come up with other theories of Israel's emergence in Palestine. While a minority of scholars, known as minimalists, believe that what we know as Israel is a late phenomenon, others believe that the roots of Israel are found in the Iron Age (followers of the immigration model and the revolution model), even if the beginnings of Israel are less developed than the biblical texts that describe the early monarchy suggest. Though they disagree on the particulars, William Dever and Israel Finkelstein point to an interesting feature of the archaeological remains at the beginning of the Iron Age (thirteenth century BC). While large Canaanite cities are shrinking in size on the coast, a few hundred small sites appear in the central hill country. These sites share a common technology for water collection (plaster-lined cisterns), olive terracing, and a surprising lack of pig bones. The suggestion is that the origins of Israel are largely an inner-Canaanite development. *See also* conquest, the; Dever, William; Finkelstein, Israel; immigration model; minimalism; revolution model.

intertestamental period *See* Second Temple Judaism.

intertextuality One of the most vibrant avenues of study these days is the relationship between biblical texts. Some studies take a diachronic approach, in that they look at how previous biblical texts inform later ones. Other studies do not ask the question of whether one text existed before another text but are interested in how texts interact and illumine each other. *See also* diachronic, synchronic.

ipsissima verba/vox Latin phrases used to refer to the record of Jesus's words. "Ipsissima verba" means the "very words" of Jesus. "Ipsissima vox" means the "very voice" or the essential message. Gospel specialists generally assert that though in most cases we don't have the exact words of Jesus (ipsissima verba), we have his authentic message (ipsissima vox). Evidence of this is that (1) Jesus taught mostly in Aramaic, yet our Gospels are in Greek; (2) Jesus's teaching is almost certainly abbreviated and summarized in the Gospels, as even his longest sermon (Matt. 5–7) would take only a few minutes to deliver; and (3) parallel accounts in the Gospels often do not agree verbatim, which suggests they are expressing the gist of what Jesus said rather than his exact words.

Irenaeus (ca. 125–202) Early church father, apologist, theologian, and bishop of Lugdunum in Gaul (Lyon, France, today). His most famous work was *Against Heresies*, a thorough refutation of gnosticism, especially as practiced by Valentinus. Irenaeus affirmed apostolic succession and claimed that the bishops' direct connection to the apostles confirmed the truth of their teaching and exposed the falsity of gnosticism. Eschatologically, Irenaeus believed in a literal millennium (thousand-year reign of Christ), which would begin at the second coming of Christ. Irenaeus was also one of the earliest and strongest defenders of the authority and value of the fourfold Gospel over against those who promoted the gnostic gospels, or who, like Tatian, sought to bring the Gospels together into a single "harmony." See also *Diatessaron*; gnosticism, *gnōsis*.

Iron Age Archaeologists divide the past into different ages according to the material used for tools and weapons. The Stone (Paleolithic, Mesolithic, and Neolithic), Copper (Chalcolithic), Bronze, and Iron Ages are relevant for the study of the OT. The Iron Age in the ancient Near East, including Israel, begins around 1200 BC and extends to 586 BC, the date of the destruction of Jerusalem at the hands of the Babylonians. The Iron Age is divided into five primary stages referred to as IA (1200–1150 BC), IB (1150–1100 BC), IIA (1100–900 BC), IIB (900–700 BC), and IIC (700–586 BC). Scholars debate whether the exodus and settlement happened during the Late Bronze or Early Iron Age. But the period of the judges, the rise of the monarchy, its division into two parts, the Assyrian defeat of the northern kingdom, and the Babylonian destruction of Jerusalem are all dated to the Iron Age. *See also* archaeology; Bronze Age.

irony In irony, surface impressions do not directly reflect reality. The plot of the book of Esther has many ironic reversals. Haman throws the lot in order to choose a day on which he and his associates might kill the Jews (Esther 3), but on that day the Jews kill their enemies instead (9:1–19). Haman built a large sharpened pole in order to impale Mordecai (5:9–14), only to be impaled himself on it (Esther 7). The biggest irony of the Bible is the rejection and crucifixion of Christ, which led not to his defeat but to his resurrection and glorification.

Israel stele *See* Merenptah/Merneptah stele.

J

Jamnia Based on statements gleaned from the Mishnah and the Talmud, scholars have surmised that after the destruction of the second temple in Jerusalem, leading rabbis of the day met in the city of Jamnia (sometimes spelled Yavneh or Javneh) to discuss the state and practice of Judaism in the light of the loss of the temple. Among other topics, these leaders dealt with objections to the authoritative status of five books in the Tanak: Esther (which never mentions God), Song of Songs (which also does not mention God and is filled with sexual imagery), Ecclesiastes (which repeats the conclusion that life is meaningless), Proverbs (which seemed to contradict itself at Prov. 26:4–5), and Ezekiel (whose vision of the eschatological temple called for the building of steps up to the altar [Ezek. 43:17], in apparent violation of the law in Exod. 20:26). According to this account the rabbis reaffirmed the holy and authoritative status of these books. Some scholars today challenge this account of Jamnia, claiming that the events described are largely apocryphal, created to defend the authority and canonization of the Hebrew text. *See also* canon; rabbinic literature; Tanak.

JEDP *See* Documentary Hypothesis.

Jeremias, Joachim (1900–1979) German Lutheran theologian and chair of NT studies at the Georg-August University of Göttingen from 1935 to 1968. Jeremias specialized in the Jewish background to the historical Jesus, and his work did much to support the general historicity of the Gospels against the skepticism of Rudolf Bultmann and his students. Among his most important works are *New Testament Theology* (1971); *Jerusalem in the Time of Jesus* (1967); *The Prayers of Jesus* (1958); *The Parables of Jesus* (1958); and *The Eucharistic Words of Jesus* (1960).

Jerome (347–420) Early church father and translator of the Vulgate, the Latin version of the Bible that became the church's standard for a thousand years. Whereas prior to Jerome's work, all translations of the OT into Latin were done from the Greek (the Septuagint), Jerome learned Hebrew from Jewish scholars and translated from the original Hebrew. *See also* Septuagint; Vulgate.

Jerusalem Bible A Roman Catholic version of the Bible first published in 1966 and inspired by the French version *Bible de Jérusalem* (1956). The project was prompted in part by an encyclical issued by Pope Pius XII in 1943 opening the way for vernacular versions based on the original Hebrew and Greek, rather than the Latin Vulgate. One distinctive of the Jerusalem Bible is that it translates the tetragrammaton (YHWH) as "Yahweh" rather than with the traditional "LORD." When a new edition of the French version appeared in 1973, the Jerusalem Bible was revised and replaced by the New Jerusalem Bible. In general these versions follow a more functional equivalent (= idiomatic) rather than formal equivalent ("literal") method of translation. *See also* formal equivalent translation; functional equivalent translation.

Jesus Seminar A group of approximately 150 biblical scholars and laypeople, founded by Robert Funk under the auspices of the Westar Institute, that met periodically in the 1980s and '90s to discuss, debate, and vote on the authenticity of words and deeds attributed to Jesus. The Seminar was controversial because of the preponderance of negative critics in its membership, its unusual voting procedure, and the provocative statements of some participants about church conspiracies to hide the truth about the real Jesus. After voting on the words and then the deeds of Jesus, the Seminar published its results in three volumes, *The Five Gospels* (1993), *The Acts of Jesus* (1998), and *The Gospel of Jesus* (1999). They concluded that approximately 18–20 percent of the Jesus material recorded in the Gospels was authentic. *See also* Crossan, John Dominic.

Johannine Comma A textual variant in 1 John 5:7–8 that reads (in the King James Version [KJV]), "For there are three that bear record *in heaven, the Father, the Word, and the Holy Ghost: and these three are one. And there are three that bear witness in earth*, the Spirit, and the water, and the blood: and these three agree in one." The words in italics appear in the Latin Vulgate but do not appear in any of our earliest Greek manuscripts. Erasmus, who produced the first printed edition of the Greek NT, left these words out of his first edition because they appeared in no Greek manuscript of which he was aware. He was heavily criticized and eventually included them in his next edition when a Greek manuscript with the variant (probably spuriously created) was presented to him. The sentence then became part of the Textus Receptus, the Greek text underlying the King James Version. *See also* Erasmus, Desiderius; King James Version (KJV); Textus Receptus.

Johannine community Designation often given to the early Christian community associated with the production and transmission of the Gospel of John and (usually) the Epistles of John. This community purportedly defined itself over against Judaism and held distinct beliefs related to Christology, the Holy Spirit / Paraclete, the Eucharist, and other issues. This theory arose in part because of the uniqueness of John in relation to the Synoptic Gospels and because of claims that the Gospel is not the work of a single individual but rather a composite that arose in stages within the life of this community.

Joseph narrative The book of Genesis is typically divided into three large parts, opening with the primeval narrative (chaps. 1–11), followed by the patriarchal narrative (chaps. 12–36), and finishing with the Joseph narrative (chaps. 37–50). The Joseph narrative is really the *toledot* ("genealogy," "generations," "descendants") of Jacob (Gen. 37:2), which means that it is an account that centers on Jacob's children, but the focus is primarily on Joseph, the one whom God uses to rescue his chosen family during a devastating famine (50:19–20). The Joseph narrative explains how the people of God came to reside in Egypt and thus provides a narrative bridge to the beginning of the book of Exodus. The style of the Joseph narrative differs from the earlier parts of Genesis, having a smooth and coherent plotline, unlike the more episodic telling of the patriarchal narratives. Some even identify the Joseph narrative as one of the first short stories in the history of literature.

Josephus (ca. AD 37–100) Jewish historian whose writings provide insight into the first-century world of Judaism and the Greco-Roman world. Josephus was born Joseph ben Matityahu into an aristocratic and priestly Jewish family. He urged his countrymen not to revolt against the Romans, but when revolution broke out in 66 he took up arms and served as a general on the Jewish side, defending Galilee. He was eventually captured, but upon surrendering to the Roman general Vespasian, he "prophesied" that Vespasian would be the next emperor of Rome. As predicted, when Emperor Nero committed suicide, Vespasian returned to Rome to become emperor. Josephus remained with Titus, Vespasian's son, as his interpreter as Titus completed the siege and destruction of Jerusalem. Josephus then returned to Rome under the patronage of Vespasian and Titus. His name was changed to Titus Flavius Josephus, and he spent the rest of his years in Rome writing on behalf of his patrons. Four of his works survive: *The History of the Jewish War*, a seven-volume account of the Jewish revolution; *The Antiquities of the Jews*, a twenty-volume work tracing the history of the Jewish people from creation to Josephus's time; *The Life of Josephus*, an autobiography; and *Against Apion*, a defense of Judaism against a pagan opponent.

Jubilee Year At the end of seven Sabbatical Year cycles, Israel was to celebrate a Jubilee Year, at which time property would be returned to its original tribal allotment, slaves would be set free, debts would be forgiven, the land would be left fallow, and God's blessings would be poured out on his people (Lev. 25:8–55). It is not certain whether this Jubilee Year was to be celebrated in the forty-ninth or the fiftieth year. Isaiah 61 applies the imagery of Jubilee to God's eschatological salvation, where a messianic herald of salvation proclaims good news to the poor and release for prisoners. In his Nazareth sermon in Luke's Gospel (Luke 4:18–30), Jesus quotes this passage in Isaiah and applies this eschatological jubilee language to himself. *See also* Sabbatical Year.

Jubilees A Jewish work, part of the Pseudepigrapha, which claims to have been delivered to Moses through angels on Mount Sinai. *Jubilees* recounts and embellishes the events of Genesis, presenting a theological chronology of history organized into divisions of sevens. Fifty Jubilees are recounted from creation to the giving of the law at Sinai. *See also* Jubilee Year; Pseudepigrapha, the.

Judah The dominant tribe in southern Israel, named after the fourth son of Jacob. Judah was the tribe of the family of David, with whom God made a covenant of kingship (2 Sam. 7), according to which his descendants would rule on the throne located in Jerusalem thereafter. After the reign of David's son Solomon, the northern tribes rejected David's descendants as their king, so after 931 BC Judah existed as an independent nation (*see* divided monarchy), also known as the southern kingdom. Judah itself lost its national status in 586 BC, when it was made a province of the Babylonian Empire.

Judaizers Designation given to Jewish Christians who asserted that Gentiles needed to keep the OT law and be circumcised (i.e., to first become Jews) in order to be saved. Paul's letter to the Galatian churches appears to be directed against the influence of Judaizers in Galatia. Similarly, Judaizers are in view in Acts 15:1, when "certain people" come down from Jerusalem to Antioch, teaching the believers there, "Unless you are circumcised according to the custom prescribed by Moses, you cannot be saved." The Jerusalem Council concluded, against the Judaizers, that Gentiles did not need to be circumcised in order to be saved but that they should keep certain stipulations so as not to offend their Jewish brothers and sisters (Acts 15:6–29). *See also* Council of Jerusalem.

Judas Maccabeus *See* Maccabees, Maccabean revolt.

judges After the death of Joshua (of disputed date but sometime between the early fourteenth and the twelfth centuries) and before the rise of kingship (ca. 1050 BC), Israel experienced a period characterized by political fragmentation, moral depravity, and spiritual confusion. According to the book of Judges, when Israel sinned, God sent a foreign ruler to oppress them (usually on a regional basis), but when Israel repented and cried out to God for help, God would raise up a judge to rescue them and establish a period of peace. These judges, at least the ones commonly called major judges (Othniel, Ehud, Shamgar, Deborah, Gideon, Jephthah, and Samson) were not judicial figures for the most part but people whom God used to forcibly evict the oppressors. Other judges, commonly called minor judges, do not have stories of rescue connected with them but seem to have had a kind of administrative authority (Tola and Jair [10:1–5]; Ibzan, Elon, and Abdon [12:8–15]).

Jülicher, Adolf (1857–1938) *See* allegory; parable.

K

Käsemann, Ernst (1906–98) German NT scholar and former student of Rudolf Bultmann. His lecture at a reunion of Bultmann's students in 1953 is generally credited with launching what was called the "new [or second] quest for the historical Jesus." Käsemann taught at the Universities of Mainz (1946–51), Göttingen (1951–59), and Tübingen (1959–71) and wrote books on NT history and theology, most notably an influential commentary on Romans. *See also* Bornkamm, Günther; Bultmann, Rudolf Karl; new (second) quest for the historical Jesus.

kenosis Greek term meaning "emptying" and referring to the incarnation of the Son of God as portrayed in Philippians 2. Paul says that Jesus did not consider equality with God something to be "held on to" or "exploited"; rather, he "emptied himself" (or, "made himself nothing") by taking the form of a servant, being made in human likeness (Phil. 2:6–7). Considerable debate concerns the question of what Jesus emptied himself. His deity? His divine attributes? Perhaps the best answer is that he gave up the right to the direct use of these divine attributes.

kerygma Greek term meaning "preaching" or "proclamation" and referring to the proclamation of the good news of salvation, the gospel message. In 1 Corinthians 15:3–4 Paul sums up the proclamation as "Christ died for our sins according to the Scriptures, . . . he was buried, . . . he was raised on the third day according to the

Scriptures." The *kērygma* is sometimes contrasted with the *didachē*. The former is the proclamation of the message of salvation, while the latter is the teaching and stories about Jesus and their significance for faith and practice. The former is the call to repentance and faith in Jesus as Savior. The latter is the catechism that follows as new believers are instructed in the faith.

Ketef Hinnom amulet In 1980 archaeologists discovered two small silver amulets in a grave dated to the sixth century BC on the Ketef Hinnom ("shoulder of [the valley of] Hinnom") in southwest Jerusalem. When unrolled, the amulets contained portions of the so-called priestly benediction of Numbers 6:24–26, making this the oldest surviving portion of Hebrew Scripture known today.

Kethib and Qere Ancient scribes—known as Masoretes—who made a new manuscript of the biblical text were intent to copy exactly what was on their exemplar (what they received from pre-Masoretic tradition), even when they felt it might not be correct. Thus, they wrote (*kethib*) what the exemplar had but then suggested a reading (*qere*) that they thought was correct. *See also* Masoretes, Masoretic Text; textual criticism.

Ketuvim The Hebrew Bible has a different order than the English OT, whose order is based on the Greek Septuagint. The Ketuvim is the third and final part of the so-called Tanak. The first part is Torah (the Law); the second is Nevi'im (the Prophets). Different ancient scrolls have different orders of books, but the Ketuvim (English: "Writings") contains Psalms, Job, Proverbs, Ruth, Song of Songs, Ecclesiastes, Lamentations, Esther, Daniel, Ezra-Nehemiah, and Chronicles. *See also* Nevi'im; Pentateuch; Septuagint.

Khirbet el-Qom inscription An inscription written on a pillar in a cave used for a burial that was found near Khirbet el-Qom, which is located about six miles to the southeast of the city of Lachish, west of Jerusalem. This inscription is dated to the end of the eighth century BC. It contains a blessing written from a person named Abiyahu to Uryahu. Though fragmentary, it is interesting because the composer blesses Uryahu to Yahweh, the God of Israel, but also mentions the Canaanite goddess Asherah. *See also* Asherah; Yahweh.

King James Version (KJV) The KJV, also known as the Authorized Version (AV), is the most popular English translation of all time. The KJV arose in the late 1500s at a time of competing Bible versions. While the bishops of the Anglican Church favored the Bishops' Bible (1568), the Puritans and other Reformers favored the Geneva Bible (1560). When King James VI of Scotland came to the British throne as James I, he called a conference at Hampton Court (1604) to address various concerns raised by Puritan clerics. Though James ended up rejecting almost all of the Puritan demands, he approved their request for a new Bible translation. His goal was likely to replace the Geneva Bible, which contained antimonarchical notes, with something more sympathetic to his royal authority. The translation was produced in seven years by forty-seven of the leading British biblical scholars of the day and was published in 1611. Though not at first universally extolled or accepted, over the next hundred years the KJV gradually superseded its competitors in the minds of English readers and became the leading English version—a position it would retain for the next three centuries.

Kingu *See* Qingu (Kingu).

kinsman-redeemer Leviticus 25:25–30 describes the responsibility of a near relative to come to the aid of a destitute relative who has had to sell their property, while 25:47–50 speaks to the situation when a relative sells themselves into slavery to a foreigner living in the land. Jeremiah 32:1–15 narrates how Jeremiah functions in this way for a relative named Hanamel. In the book of Ruth, Boaz acts as such a redeemer (Heb. *go'el*) toward Ruth when he marries her after the death of her first husband, a relative of his (Ruth 3:9, 12–13). In Genesis 38, after the death of Judah's firstborn son, who was married to Tamar, who had not yet had a child, Judah tells his second son, "Perform your duty as her brother-in-law and produce offspring for your brother" (v. 8). While the Levitical law does not specifically talk about this duty, it appears that the kinsman-redeemer had a number of different obligations, including the brother-in-law (or closest relative) who marries a woman whose husband has died and left her childless (such a marriage was known as a levirate, from the Latin term for brother-in-law).

Kittel, Gerhard (1888–1948) Protestant German biblical scholar and lexicographer. Kittel is best known for editing the massive theological wordbook *Theologisches Wörterbuch zum Neuen Testament*, translated into English as *Theological Dictionary of the New Testament*. Though a highly significant work of NT historical and theological scholarship, the dictionary was severely criticized by James Barr and others for its frequent confusion of words and ideas. Though categorized according to Greek words, the articles in the dictionary are often related to the history of ideas and theological concepts rather than to lexicography per se. And there is significant confusion between these two. In recent years Kittel's strong anti-Semitism and support for the Nazis have also been highlighted and criticized. *See also* Barr, James.

Koine Greek The conquests of Alexander the Great in the fourth century BC made Greek the lingua franca, or common trade language, of the Eastern Mediterranean region. *Koinē*, or "common" Greek (also called Hellenistic Greek), refers to the language used for politics, trade, and commerce among the diverse peoples of these regions. It would generally be second-language Greek; people would speak their own native tongue with their own people and use Greek in their interaction with outsiders.

koinōnia Greek term often translated "fellowship" but also as "partnership," "participation," and "sharing." The early church in Jerusalem met together and "devoted themselves to the apostles' teaching, to the fellowship [*koinōnia*], to the breaking of bread, and to prayer" (Acts 2:42). Paul thanks God for the Philippian church's "partnership [*koinōnia*] in the gospel from the first day until now"

(Phil. 1:5). In contexts like these, *koinōnia* means "striving together as one to accomplish God's purposes."

Kothar waHasis   A Canaanite deity known from the Ugaritic religious texts. His name means "skilled and wise," and his function within the pantheon was as a craftsman. Baal calls on him to create weapons for Baal's fight against the sea god Yam, and then later Baal asks him to construct a house for Baal that celebrates his kingship. *See also* Baal texts; Ugaritic.

Kugel, James   (1945–) American-born Jewish scholar of the Hebrew Bible; he has taught at Yale University, Harvard University, and Bar Ilan University. Kugel's early book *The Idea of Biblical Poetry* (1981) reshaped scholarly understanding of the workings of Hebrew parallelism, noting that the second part of a bicolon did not simply repeat the thought of the first colon but intensified or sharpened it. Kugel also made a great contribution to the study of inner-biblical interpretation and early interpretation of biblical texts, focusing in particular on Second Temple interpretation. *See also* parallelism; poetry.

Kuntillet 'Ajrud inscriptions   In 1970 at the site of Kuntillet 'Ajrud in northeastern Sinai archaeologists discovered two large jars (*pithoi*) with inscriptions and crude drawings (graffiti) that bear interest for the study of the OT. These artifacts are dated to somewhere around the end of the ninth and early eighth centuries BC. The most striking picture is a stick drawing of two horned deities, one male and one female. While some argue that the depiction is of the Egyptian god Bes, it is more likely to be connected to a nearby inscription that refers to Yahweh and "his asherah," which either is a reference to the goddess Asherah or should be translated "his wife." If this is correct, then this would attest to the kind of pagan practices condemned by the prophets.

Kyrios   Greek term commonly translated "lord." It was used in the Septuagint, the Greek OT, as a translation for both the Hebrew *adonai* ("lord," "master," "sir") and for the Tetragrammaton (YHWH or Yahweh), the divine name for God. When applied to Jesus in the NT, it often carries divine connotations. Also significant is the fact that Roman citizens demonstrated their allegiance to the emperor by affirming that "Caesar is Lord [*kyrios*]." To declare "Jesus is Lord" could be tantamount to sedition. *See also* Tetragrammaton; Yahweh.

L

L source *See* Synoptic problem.

Lachish letters About nine letters discovered during excavations at ancient Lachish, written in Hebrew with ink on ostraca from a military person named Hoshaiah to the commander of the garrison at Lachish named Yaush. The date is most likely during the Babylonian invasion of Judah around 596 BC. Interestingly, there is a mention of a "prophet" as well as worry that they cannot see the "signal fires" of the nearby city of Azekah, which may indicate that it had been captured.

Ladd, George Eldon (1911–82) American NT scholar whose works like *The Presence of the Future* (1974) and *A Theology of the New Testament* (1974) developed the view of "inaugurated eschatology," a middle ground between "realized" and "future" (or "imminent") eschatology. Inaugurated eschatology claims that the kingdom Jesus proclaimed was both "already" and "not yet." It has arrived through the life, death, and resurrection of Jesus but will be consummated in an earthly kingdom at some time in the future. Ladd, who taught at Fuller Theological Seminary, was a proponent of historic premillennialism, an eschatological position between dispensational premillennialism and Reformed amillennialism. *See also* amillennialism; Cullmann, Oscar; dispensationalism; Dodd, Charles Harold.

lectio divina A Latin expression meaning "divine reading" (or "spiritual reading"). The practice involves the reading of and meditation on Scripture in order to promote a deeper, more personal level of communion with God. The practice has its roots in the Benedictine Order and historically involves four "moments" or steps: *lectio* ("reading"), *meditatio* ("meditation"), *oratio* ("prayer"), and *contemplatio* ("reflection" or "contemplation").

lectionary In Jewish and Christian traditions, a book or collection containing Scripture readings to be used in the course of a religious calendar or for special days or occasions. The set readings of a particular church or denomination are known as its liturgy. The early Greek lectionaries are important to the field of textual criticism, since they provide an important witness to the Greek text of the NT. *See also* textual criticism.

leitmotiv A German term meaning "leading motif" or "chief theme." For example, the leitmotiv of John's Gospel might be described as the self-revelation of the Father through the Son. The term is also used of important recurrent themes that are not necessarily the central theme. We may say, for example, that an important leitmotiv in Luke's Gospel is God's concern for the poor and outcast.

Levenson, Jon D. (1949–) Hebrew Bible scholar and longtime professor at Harvard Divinity School (1988 to the present). His writings have been extremely influential in the areas of biblical theology, including the relationship between Jewish and Christian theology, the literary approach to biblical interpretation, and the book of Genesis (with a focus on Abraham). He also has focused on biblical interpretation during the Second Temple period and early rabbinic exegesis. *See also* biblical theology.

levirate marriage *See* kinsman-redeemer.

lex talionis Latin for "law of the talion," the talion being retribution. In biblical studies, it refers to the principle that the punishment for a crime must be commensurate with the crime. While stated in physical terms, "life for life, eye for eye, tooth for tooth, hand for hand, foot for foot, burn for burn, bruise for bruise, wound for wound" (Exod. 21:23b–25; see also Lev. 24:19–21), it was not literally applied and would be considered a maximum penalty. This law, while sometimes pilloried as primitive, actually restrains punishment of the type envisioned by Lamech the descendant of Cain—who said, "I killed a man for wounding me" (Gen. 4:23)—and is the principle that governs penalties today even in modern societies like the United States.

literary criticism In its most general sense, "literary criticism" refers to the examination, analysis, and critique of literature. In biblical studies, the term is used in various ways: (1) It can refer to the study of biblical genres in terms of their nature, sources, composition, and authorship. Used in this sense, it is roughly synonymous with "historical criticism." (2) More recently, the term has been used to refer to the examination of the text as a whole, focusing on its narrative and rhetorical functions. In this sense it is a counterpart to "historical criticism" and refers to methodologies like narrative criticism and rhetorical criticism that examine the literary features of a text apart from its sources or history of composition. *See also* historical criticism; narrative criticism.

Living Bible, The Highly idiomatic translation of the Bible produced by Kenneth Taylor and published in 1971. The version has its origins in Taylor's family devotions. His children had trouble understanding literal Bible versions, so Taylor began paraphrasing readings from the American Standard Version (ASV; 1901). Taylor published the NT letters in 1962 as *Living Letters*. Billy Graham received a copy and was so impressed that he published fifty thousand copies and used it in his evangelistic crusades. The translation's highly readable and engaging style resulted in great success. By 1997, forty million copies of *The Living Bible* had been sold. A major revision was produced in 1996, known as the New Living Translation (NLT). *See also* New Living Translation (NLT).

lower criticism *See* textual criticism.

Luke-Acts Term coined by H. J. Cadbury to refer to Luke's two-volume work, the Gospel of Luke and the book of Acts. The designation is intended to stress the literary and theological unity between these two books. Cadbury was a pioneer in the literary analysis of Luke's writings.

LXX *See* Septuagint.

M

M source *See* Synoptic problem.

Maccabees, Maccabean revolt Insurrectionist movement launched in 166 BC by Jewish patriots against the attempts by the Seleucid ruler Antiochus IV "Epiphanes" to suppress Judaism. Antiochus's earlier attempts to gain the loyalty of his Jewish subjects against his Egyptian rivals, the Ptolemies, were met by strong opposition from Jewish conservatives. This resulted in increasing imposition of pagan religion in Judea and restrictions on Judaism. Ultimately, Antiochus banned circumcision and adherence to the law of Moses and offered pagan sacrifices in the Jerusalem temple (the abomination of desolation). In the Judean village of Modein, a Jewish priest named Mattathias was ordered by a Seleucid official to offer a pagan sacrifice. He refused and killed both the official and a Jewish sympathizer. Mattathias and his sons fled into the wilderness, from where they launched a guerrilla war. After Mattathias died, his son Judas led the revolt. Judas was given the Aramaic nickname "Maccabeus" ("the hammer") because of his prowess in battle, and the revolt took its name from this term. After various setbacks and victories, Judas successfully took Jerusalem, cleansing and rededicating the temple. The festival of Hanukkah celebrates this victory. The Maccabees ruled in Israel as priest-kings until Rome conquered Palestine in 63 BC. The story of the revolt is told in 1 Maccabees, which is part of the Apocrypha. *See also* abomination of desolation; Apocrypha, the; Hanukkah; Hasmoneans.

Magnificat Latin title given to Mary's song of praise in Luke 1:46–55. The word means "magnifies" and is the first word of the Latin version of the hymn. The Magnificat is one of four hymns in Luke's infancy narrative, all of which pick up key Lukan themes. The others are Zechariah's Benedictus (1:68–79), the angels' Gloria in Excelsis (2:14), and Simeon's Nunc Dimittis (2:29–32). The Magnificat comes after the annunciation of Jesus's birth to Mary by the angel Gabriel (1:30–35) and is given on the occasion of Mary's visit to her relative Elizabeth, who will give birth to John the Baptist. Its language recalls the prayer of Hannah in 1 Samuel 2, and its main themes are God's love and concern for the poor and humble, his humiliation of the rich and powerful, and his faithfulness to his covenant people Israel.

Major Prophets Includes the books of Isaiah, Jeremiah, and Ezekiel. The term "major," as opposed to "minor," has to do with their size. In the Hebrew Bible, the Major and the Minor Prophets are together known as the Latter Prophets, the second part of the Nevi'im. *See also* Minor Prophets; Nevi'im.

majuscule *See* uncial.

Maranatha Transliteration of an Aramaic phrase meaning either "Our Lord, come!" (*marana tha*) or "Our Lord has come!" (*maran atha*). It is used by Paul in 1 Corinthians 16:22 and also appears in the *Didache* (10:6), a church manual probably from the late first century AD. The phrase is also likely behind the Greek of Revelation 22:20. The significance is that it confirms that the early Aramaic-speaking church in Judea referred to Jesus with the exalted title "lord." It also suggests that they expected him to one day return as Savior and Judge. See also *Didache*.

Marcion of Sinope (ca. 85–160) Early church leader and theologian who denied the true incarnation of the Son (that God became a human being) and his atoning death on the cross. Marcion's gnostic-like beliefs resulted in a rejection of the material world as evil. Salvation comes not through the sacrifice of Christ but through esoteric knowledge (gnosis). He rejected Judaism as a false religion and viewed the god of the OT (called the demiurge) as an inferior, jealous tribal deity and the creator of the material universe. Marcion developed a truncated canon of Scripture, which contained only portions of the Gospel of Luke and of the Pauline Letters. Marcion's canon provided impetus for the church to respond with its own discussions on the parameters of the canon. *See also* canon; gnosticism, *gnōsis*.

Marduk The king of the Babylonian pantheon. In the Enuma Elish, Marduk assumes the kingship of the gods by defeating Tiamat and using her corpse to build the cosmos. He is the creator of humanity as well. *See also* Enuma Elish.

Mari Ancient Mari (Tel Hariri in eastern Syria on the middle Euphrates) was excavated starting in 1933. Founded in the early third millennium BC, it is important for biblical studies partly because it has produced a number of cuneiform tablets that speak of social customs that relate to the patriarchal narratives. One text, for instance, describes a ritual in which two individuals walk together through divided animal bodies in order to swear loyalty to each other. This custom has been compared to the ritual in which God in the form of a flaming torch in a smoking firepot passes through divided animal corpses to swear to Abraham that he will keep his promise to provide him with an heir (Gen. 15).

Marxist interpretation A variety of approaches to Scripture that interpret the text from the perspective of class struggle, as developed in the ideologies of Karl Marx (1818–83). Marxist interpretations are a form of liberation theology, calling for a classless society and the liberation of the masses from the oppressive rich, powerful, and elite. Within Marxist criticism, the Bible is sometimes viewed as a means of liberation and sometimes as a tool of oppression.

masorah Refers to notations that were added by Jewish scribes in the margins and at the end of biblical books. Their purpose was to aid in the careful preservation of the biblical books as they were copied and transmitted through time. *See also* Masoretes, Masoretic Text; textual criticism.

Masoretes, Masoretic Text The Masoretes were scribes who worked from the fourth to the tenth century AD to transmit the text of the Hebrew Bible from one generation to another. They standardized the text, copying one text tradition and thus suppressing others. They also added vowels (vocalization) plus special marks (accentuation) that showed the relationship between words. *See also* textual criticism.

maximalism A term, sometimes but not always pejorative, used to refer to scholars who believe that the OT contains reliable historical information. Maximalist scholars are at the opposite end of the spectrum from minimalists. *See also* minimalism.

Meier, John P. (1942–) American Roman Catholic scholar and priest who has specialized in historical-Jesus studies. His magnum opus is a five-volume work entitled *A Marginal Jew: Rethinking the Historical Jesus* (1991, 1994, 2001, 2009, 2016). Meier seeks to reach conclusions with a strict historical methodology, using the criteria of authenticity to determine the historicity of each Gospel pericope. Meier concludes that Jesus is best viewed as an eschatological prophet and that the kingdom he proclaimed had both present and future dimensions. *See also* criteria of authenticity.

Merenptah/Merneptah stele As the name implies, a stele set up by Pharaoh Merenptah (1213–1203 BC). It commemorated his victories in Canaan. Discovered in Egypt in 1896, it is usually dated to 1209/1208 BC and contains the oldest extrabiblical mention of Israel. It is also called the Israel stele. *See also* Egypt; stele, stela.

merism Merism most commonly refers to the citation of two poles to indicate everything in between. "From Dan [in the far north] to Beersheba [in the far south]" (1 Kings 4:25) means the entirety of Israel. When Job is afflicted with painful sores "from the soles of his feet to the top of his head" (Job 2:7), that means that every part of his body was afflicted with disease. Similarly, the phrase "heaven and earth" (Ps. 69:34) means the entire cosmos.

Mesopotamia Greek for "between two rivers" and referring to the alluvial plain that lies between the Tigris and Euphrates Rivers. Today it is known as Iraq, but in antiquity it was the location of Sumer (in the south during the fourth and third millennia) and then Babylon (in the south) and Assyria (in the north) during the second millennium and first half of the first millennium. *See also* Assyria; Babylon; Sumer.

Message, The A popular version of the Bible produced by Eugene Peterson, with various scholars serving as translation consultants. The NT was published in 1993, and the whole Bible in 2002. The version could perhaps better be called a "transculturation" than a translation. Whereas a traditional translation seeks to take the reader back into the world of the text, *The Message* brings the message of the text into a contemporary context. Peterson's goal was to translate the tone, rhythm, and content of the Bible into the way people speak and think today. The translation's colorful and engaging style has made it a popular supplement to more traditional versions.

messianic secret A major theme in Mark's Gospel, as Jesus repeatedly seeks to keep his identity as the Messiah a secret. He silences demons who cry out that he is the Son of God (1:24–26, 34; 3:11–12); he tells those he heals not to let anyone know what he has done (1:44; 5:43; 7:36; 8:26); and when Peter confesses that Jesus is the Messiah, Jesus tells the disciples not to tell this to anyone (8:30; 9:9). The motif was made famous in the early twentieth century by William Wrede (1859–1906), who claimed that the messianic secret was a literary and theological device used by Mark to cover up Jesus's unmessianic life. According to Wrede, Mark found little in the tradition to identify Jesus as the Messiah, so he picked up and expanded this motif that Jesus was the Messiah but that he kept this a secret until after the resurrection. Wrede's view—that Mark's theological agenda, rather than historical concerns, is driving his story—has had a profound impact on Gospel studies. Yet Wrede's conclusions about Mark's purposes are unlikely, not least because although Jesus tries to keep his identity a secret, those he cautions often proclaim it anyway. It is more likely that the messianic secret was Jesus's way of tamping down the political expectations people had about the Messiah. Jesus calls for silence so that he can define his messianic role on his own terms.

metaphor A figure of speech that compares two things that are essentially unlike except in some specific sense. "The LORD is my shepherd" is a metaphor—it is literally untrue but figuratively rich in that it intends to teach us about God by comparing God with a shepherd. There are many ways in which God is not like a shepherd, but as shepherds guide, protect, and provide for the sheep under their care, so God guides, protects, and provides for the psalmist. Simile differs from metaphor since the former uses the word "like" or "as," thus lessening the shock of the comparison. *See also* simile.

meter In certain poetic traditions, poets wrote utilizing a set rhythm, or recurring pattern of sound. In classical Latin poetry, meter is a repeated pattern of stressed and unstressed syllables. The existence of meter in Hebrew poetry has long been debated. Augustine (fourth–fifth century AD) believed that biblical poetry contained meter similar to that found in classical poetry. More recently others have suggested that meter may be detected by counting syllables in the poetic line. Today most scholars doubt that Hebrew poetry has meter. *See also* poetry.

metonymy While metaphor is figurative language created by analogy or comparison, metonymy is figurative language created by association. Perhaps the best known type of metonymy is called synecdoche, which is part for a whole. When the poet says in reference to God, "your rod and your staff—they comfort me" (Ps. 23:4), he refers to objects that are associated with the guiding and protecting functions of the shepherd. *See also* metaphor; synecdoche.

Metzger, Bruce M. (1914–2007) American NT scholar and textual critic. Metzger taught at Princeton Theological Seminary for forty-six years, from 1938 to 1984, and then served as professor emeritus. He wrote prolifically on issues of textual criticism, versions of the Bible, and the development of the canon. Metzger sat on the translation committee for the United Bible Societies' Greek NT and wrote the *Textual Commentary* explaining the committee's textual choices. He was also chairman of the translation committee for the New Revised Standard Version. *See also* canon; New Revised Standard Version (NRSV); textual criticism.

midrash A genre of Jewish literature that provides rabbinic commentary, interpretation, and illustration to passages of Scripture. The noun comes from the verb *darash*, which means "to seek, inquire, study." The midrashim (pl.) date from about the fifth century to the twelfth century. While some midrash comments on legal material (halakah), most concerns nonlegal material (haggadah). The latter kind often includes expansions and embellishments of the biblical text. Some scholars have claimed that certain passages in the NT, such as the birth narratives in Matthew and Luke, are midrash rather than history, embellishing on the life of Jesus with fanciful legends. *See also* haggadah; halakah.

minimalism A term, sometimes used pejoratively, referring to those scholars who argue that the OT contains very little, if any, reliable historical information. They are thus on the opposite end of the spectrum from maximalists (*see* maximalism).There are differences among minimalist scholars, but most think that the OT is the product of a late time (Persian or even Greek period). These late writers essentially created the history of Israel (particularly the period before Josiah in the seventh century BC).

Minor Prophets Includes twelve books: Hosea, Joel, Amos, Obadiah, Jonah, Micah, Nahum, Habakkuk, Zephaniah, Haggai,

Zechariah, and Malachi. These books are called "minor" because of their relative brevity in comparison to the Major Prophets. The Minor and the Major Prophets are together known as the Latter Prophets, the second part of the Nevi'im, in the Hebrew Bible. *See also* Major Prophets; Nevi'im.

minuscule A Greek style of writing that developed in the ninth and tenth centuries and came to replace the uncial text. Minuscule letters are similar to modern Greek lowercase letters. *See also* uncial.

Mishnah *See* rabbinic literature.

Moabite Stone In 1868 a black basalt stone was discovered on which was written an inscription that features King Mesha of Moab (2 Kings 3:4) as well as Omri, king of Israel (882–871 BC), and is dated around 835 BC. Mesha remembers the time that Omri successfully subjugated Moab, but then Mesha successfully rebelled against Omri's "son," whom the biblical account identifies as Jehoram (851–842 BC). After this inscription was first discovered, local people broke it into pieces, but fortunately a squeeze (three-dimensional paper impression) had been made of the whole and a number of the pieces were recovered and reassembled. A translation may be found in *COS* 2:137–38.

monocolon *See* colon, cola.

morpheme A linguistic term meaning the smallest grammatical unit of a language. For example, the word *running* has two morphemes, the verb "run" and the participial ending "-ing." The word "wanted" has two morphemes, the verb "want" and the past-tense ending "-ed." Every word is composed of one or more morphemes.

morphology In linguistics, morphology (from the Greek *morphē*, "form") is the study of the grammatical forms of a language. For example, the verb "to be" takes on different forms depending on its person and tense: I *am* (first-person sg.); you *are* (second-person sg.); he/she/it *is* (third-person sg.); we *are* (first-person pl.); you *are* (second-person pl.); they *are* (third-person pl.). These changes in form are known as *inflection*.

Mowinckel, Sigmund (1884–1965) Norwegian OT scholar. He was a student of Hermann Gunkel and further developed Gunkel's form-critical approach to the OT, particularly the Psalms. Mowinckel was a specialist in OT ritual, most known for his argument that the book of Psalms was the hymnbook of the second temple and served as a libretto of an annual New Year's festival that celebrated the kingship of Yahweh. *See also* Akitu Festival; form criticism (*Formgeschichte*); Gunkel, Hermann.

Muilenburg, James (1896–1974) American OT scholar. He was a major influence—in the 1960s and '70s in particular—in the development of a literary approach to biblical interpretation that treated biblical books as literary, if not compositional, wholes. He explored the literary conventions used in the writing of narratives and poetry in Hebrew. *See also* narrative criticism.

multiple attestation, criterion of *See* criteria of authenticity.

Muratorian Canon Also known as the Muratorian Fragment, this manuscript contains the earliest known canonical list, including twenty-two of the twenty-seven NT writings. The fragment is a seventh-century Latin manuscript, but internal indications suggest the text was originally written in Greek around 170–80. The list includes the four Gospels, all thirteen letters of Paul, two of the three letters of John, Jude, and Revelation. Missing from the list are Hebrews, 1 and 2 Peter, James, and either 2 or 3 John (it is not clear which). The manuscript was discovered by Italian historian Ludovico Muratori in the Ambrosian Library in northern Italy and was published in 1740. *See also* canon.

mystery religions A variety of Greco-Roman religious traditions that had in common emotional excess and secret initiatory and cultic rituals. There were two main groups of mystery religions, the older, Greek mysteries (e.g., the Eleusinian mysteries, the cult of Dionysus, the Orphic mysteries) and the Eastern imports (e.g., Cybele and Attis from Phrygia, Adonis and Atargatis from Syria, Isis-Osiris and Serapis from Egypt, and Mithraism from Persia). Though diverse, these mystery religions had certain things in common. Nearly all were originally fertility or vegetation rites centered on local deities whose myths were reflected in the religions' initiations and other celebrations. Nearly all had the motif of a dying and rising god. This idea did not come from the death and resurrection of a historical figure, as in Christianity, but from the natural seasonal course of nature. All tended to be highly emotional, with little emphasis on the intellect or on moral or ethical behavior. Initiation was a matter of seeing and participating rather than of believing and accomplishing. The chief goal was to attain immortality by partaking mystically with the god through the passage from death to life. Strict exclusivity and secrecy were practiced. No one but the initiated could be present at the services, and knowledge of what was done was considered too sacred to be shared with outsiders. This does not mean that these religions were exclusive societies that only certain classes could join. Membership seemed for the most part to be open to any who chose to be initiated, a fact that greatly increased their appeal.

It has sometimes been argued that features of the mystery religions influenced early Christian beliefs and practices, including divine sonship, the Eucharist, and resurrection faith. Such parallels are much less accepted today than during the heyday of the history of religions school in the early twentieth century. *See also* history of religions school (*Religionsgeschichtliche Schule*).

myth, mythology The term "myth" is a notoriously slippery one used in multiple ways. In popular imagination, myths are simply made-up stories having no connection to reality, but that is not typically how biblical scholarship uses the term. Sometimes "myth" is used to designate any story about the divine realm as opposed to epic and legend, which are stories about heroic humans. Another understanding of myths is that they are stories of origins and explain why the world is as it is. This definition says nothing about whether or not myths are fictional or factual—that is, actually occurring in space and time. Myth develops and grounds a worldview. As stories of origins, myths look back into the distant past. As stories of foundation, myths, unsurprisingly, have as their main character(s) deity; however, the presence of humanity does not necessarily disqualify a text from being considered a member of the genre myth. *See also* epic.

N

Nag Hammadi Library A collection of fifty-two (mostly) gnostic texts discovered in 1945 in Nag Hammadi, a town in Upper Egypt. The texts, contained in twelve leather-bound papyrus codices, were written in Coptic and have provided an important window into the second-century movement known as gnosticism. Of the fifty-two texts, perhaps the most significant for NT scholars was the *Gospel of Thomas*, which is widely viewed as the earliest and most important of the noncanonical gospels. Also significant is the *Gospel of Mary*, since it provides information concerning gnostic views related to women. *See also* gnosticism, *gnōsis*; *Gospel of Thomas*.

narrative criticism Methodology that examines the narrative literature of the Bible as "story" and uses contemporary categories developed for the analysis of the novel and other narrative literature. Narrative criticism of the NT arose in the 1970s and '80s, especially as a corrective to the atomistic approaches of historical criticism (source, form, and redaction criticism), which examined the history and development of the text rather than viewing it as a literary whole. For most narrative critics, the final form of the text is all that matters. Narrative critics study plot, characters, and settings within the narrative world of the text. They speak of implied authors (the author as discerned from the narrative alone), narrators (the voice one hears telling the story), and implied readers (an imaginary reader who responds appropriately to the narrative strategy). They also examine the many literary devices—repetition, inclusio, chiasm, intercalation, foreshadowing, and so on—used to carry the story forward. *See also* implied author; implied reader.

narrator *See* implied author.

Nephilim The first mention of Nephilim comes in Genesis 6:4, where they are the offspring of the "sons of God" and the "daughters of men." They are described as "heroes of old, men of renown" (NIV). This text is one of the most enigmatic passages in all of Scripture, and thus proper caution should be exercised in interpreting it. There are questions about the identity of the sons of God (angels, people from the line of Seth, powerful lords) and the daughters of men (human women, people from the line of Cain, lower-class women) and about the identity of the Nephilim (the term means "falling ones"), their offspring. The fact that a later tribe of people of "great size" are given the name (Num. 13:33) may signify that these earlier Nephilim were tall.

Nestle-Aland text *See* critical text.

Nevi'im (sometimes spelled Nebi'im or Neviim) The second of three parts of the Hebrew Bible (*see also* Ketuvim; Pentateuch). Nevi'im is translated "Prophets" and may be divided into two parts, the Former Prophets (Joshua, Judges, Samuel, and Kings) and the Latter Prophets (Isaiah, Jeremiah, Ezekiel, and the Twelve Minor Prophets).

New American Standard Bible (NASB) A revision of the American Standard Version (ASV), produced by the Lockman Foundation of La Habra, California. The NASB was initiated in part because some conservatives perceived the Revised Standard Version (RSV) as liberal. The NT of the NASB was published in 1963, and the full Bible in 1971. A revision was released in 1995. The NASB is one of the most formally equivalent ("literal") English versions available today. *See also* formal equivalent translation.

new hermeneutic Movement that began in the mid-1960s, especially through the work of Ernst Fuchs and Gerhard Ebeling, who in turn were influenced by the philosophical framework of Martin Heidegger and the existentialist biblical scholar Rudolf Bultmann. The new hermeneutic acknowledges the historical position of the text and the legitimacy of historical-critical methods but also affirms the social and cultural gap between the original readers and the modern readers and the subjective and culture-bound viewpoint of the interpreter. Each reading of the text represents a new and unique language event and an existential encounter with the word. *See also* Bultmann, Rudolf Karl; historical criticism.

New International Version (NIV) A new Bible version (not a revision) sponsored by the New York Bible Society (subsequently called the International Bible Society and now Biblica). The NT appeared in 1973, and the full Bible in 1978. A revision was released in 1984 and again in 2011. The translation was originally done by approximately one hundred biblical scholars and is maintained by the fifteen-member Committee on Bible Translation. The NIV was the first contemporary English version to eclipse the King James Version (KJV) in sales. Its popularity is due in part to its mediating translation philosophy, somewhere between formal and functional equivalence. *See also* formal equivalent translation; functional equivalent translation; King James Version (KJV).

New Jerusalem Bible (NJB) *See* Jerusalem Bible.

New Jewish Publication Society (NJPS) translation of the Jewish Bible A modern translation of the Hebrew Scriptures (the Christian OT). Previously referred to as the New Jewish Version (NJV), this version was published by the Jewish Publication Society in parts, beginning in 1969 and being completed in 1985. It replaces the 1917 version of the Jewish Publication Society (abbreviated JPS). The NJPS is not a revision, however, but a completely new translation from the Hebrew. (The old JPS was an adaptation of the Revised Version and the American Standard Version.) The text follows the Hebrew order of books rather than that found in most English versions (which follow the order of the Greek Septuagint).

The Hebrew order is Torah (the five books of Moses), Nevi'im (Prophets), and Ketuvim (Writings); hence the acronym Tanak (*Tanakh* in the title of the NJPS edition). *See also* Tanak.

New King James Version (NKJV) A revision of the King James Version (KJV) initiated by Arthur Farstad and sponsored by Thomas Nelson Publishers of Nashville, TN. The NT was published in 1979, and the full Bible in 1982. The NKJV is unique among contemporary Bible versions in that it follows the Textus Receptus, the Greek text that lies behind the KJV. Footnotes in the NKJV alert readers to places where the Textus Receptus differs from either the majority of manuscripts (Majority Text) or the critical Greek text utilized by most other English versions (UBS Greek NT; Nestle-Aland Greek NT). The NKJV is one of the most formally equivalent ("literal") versions among contemporary English versions. *See also* formal equivalent translation; King James Version (KJV); Textus Receptus.

New Living Translation (NLT) A totally new translation in the tradition of *The Living Bible* (1971), published in 1996. A new edition of the NLT followed in 2004. While *The Living Bible* was the work of one person, Kenneth Taylor, the NLT was a committee work involving eighty-seven scholars from a variety of denominations. *The Living Bible* was a paraphrase, meaning a simplification of another English version—the American Standard Version (ASV). The NLT, though following the idiomatic spirit of *The Living Bible*, is an original translation from the Hebrew and Greek. Its translation methodology is dynamic equivalence (now more commonly referred to as functional equivalence), meaning it seeks the closest natural equivalent in English for Hebrew and Greek words and phrases. *See also* formal equivalent translation; functional equivalent translation; *Living Bible, The.*

new perspective on Paul A scholarly movement away from a traditional perspective on Pauline soteriology, especially as explicated by the Protestant Reformers. The movement was initiated by E. P.

Sanders in his work *Paul and Palestinian Judaism* (1977). Sanders argued that the Judaism of Jesus's day was not legalistic and governed by works righteousness, as the apostle Paul claimed. It was rather a religion of grace. God graciously chose Israel and made a covenant with the nation. Obedience to the law was not a means of salvation, which came by grace, but was rather the means by which Israel *maintained* its covenant relationship with God. Sanders coined the term "covenantal nomism" to describe this perspective. Paul, Sanders claimed, came to believe that Jesus was the Messiah. If Jesus was the way of salvation, then the Jewish law could not be. As Sanders put it, Paul argues backwards, *from solution to plight.* The solution is that Jesus is the Messiah and Savior. If this is true, there must be a problem with Israel's present situation (the plight). Paul claims this problem is legalism. Israel is trying to be saved by works.

Sanders's perspective has been picked up and modified by others. J. D. G. Dunn and N. T. Wright, for example, argue that Sanders is essentially right about Judaism, but wrong about Paul. The "works of the law" that Paul rejects are not legalistic works trying to earn righteousness. They are, rather, the "identity markers" (or, "boundary markers") of what it means to be Jewish, including circumcision, Sabbath observance, and dietary laws. Paul is essentially arguing that you don't need to become Jewish in order to become a Christ follower. Scholarship today runs the gamut, from those who reject outright the new perspective on Paul to those who accept it in whole or in part. *See also* Wright, Nicholas Thomas.

New Revised Standard Version (NRSV) A revision of the Revised Standard Version (RSV) produced under the auspices of the National Council of Churches and published in 1990. Princeton NT professor Bruce Metzger served as the chairman of the translation committee. The NRSV follows the translation philosophy of the RSV, which is generally formal equivalent. The NRSV was one of the first English Bible versions to consistently utilize gender-inclusive language for masculine generics in Hebrew and Greek. The NRSV is one of the most popular versions among academics in the field of biblical studies. *See also* formal equivalent translation; Revised Standard Version (RSV).

new (second) quest for the historical Jesus Movement launched in the early 1950s by Ernst Käsemann and other former students of Rudolf Bultmann. Whereas Bultmann's skepticism had resulted in a nearly complete rejection of the search for the historical Jesus (in favor of an existential encounter with the Christ of faith), these former students (now professors) asserted that the quest was legitimate and that it was possible to say *something* historically about the identity of Jesus. Yet because they were operating from the same modernist worldview and antisupernatural skepticism as Bultmann, the portrait of Jesus most of these scholars found was minimalistic. For most, Jesus was little more than a failed apocalyptic prophet. *See also* Bornkamm, Günther; Bultmann, Rudolf Karl; Käsemann, Ernst; quest for the historical Jesus; third quest for the historical Jesus.

Nile River The longest river in the world (ca. 4,150 miles), it begins in the mountainous region of central Africa and flows northward, eventually through Egypt, where at its northernmost point it divides into many channels (the so-called Nile Delta) that flow into the Mediterranean Sea. Every year after the snow melts in the mountains of central Africa, the Nile floods, spreading good soil through the valley. Beginning in antiquity, the floodwaters were extended by irrigation projects. This feature of the Nile allowed for the surplus that funded the development of early civilization in the Nile Valley beginning at the end of the fourth millennium BC. Due to the flow of the Nile from the south to the north, southern Egypt is called Upper Egypt and northern Egypt is called Lower Egypt. *See also* Egypt.

nomina sacra Latin for "sacred names" and referring to the practice, followed by early copyists of the Greek Bible, of abbreviating divine names, usually with the first and last letter of the name. For example, "God" (ΘΕΟΣ, *theos*) would be abbreviated ΘΣ (*ths*), and

"Jesus Christ" (ΙΗΣΟΥΣ ΧΡΙΣΤΟΣ, *Iēsous Christos*) would be abbreviated ΙΣ ΧΣ (*Is Chs*). A line would be drawn across the top of the abbreviation to identify it as a *nomen sacrum* (sg.).

northern kingdom Upon the death of Solomon (ca. 931 BC), the ten northern tribes rejected his son, Rehoboam, as king and proclaimed Jeroboam, a former official in Solomon's cabinet who had been a political refugee in Egypt, as their ruler. This kingdom lasted until the Assyrians defeated them in 722 BC.

Northwest Semitic A branch of Semitic languages that includes Hebrew and languages that, in terms of their linguistic structure, are most similar to Hebrew. These include Eblaite, Ugaritic, Aramaic, and a number of other, less frequently attested languages like Moabite. Northwest Semitic is more distantly related to South Semitic (Arabic) and East Semitic (Akkadian) languages. The closer a language is to Hebrew, the more helpful it is for our understanding of Hebrew. *See also* Akkadian; Arabic; Aram, Aramaic; Eblaite; Hebrew language; Ugaritic.

Noth, Martin (1902–68) German OT scholar in the mid-twentieth century. Along with Gerhard von Rad he utilized tradition-historical criticism in the study of the Bible. He studied the historical traditions closely and was an architect of the theory that Samuel-Kings developed a Deuteronomic perspective on the history of Israel. He also helped develop the immigration theory of Israel's entry into the promised land. *See also* Deuteronomic/Deuteronomistic History; immigration model; tradition-historical criticism; von Rad, Gerhard.

Nunc Dimittis Latin title given to Simeon's song of praise in Luke 2:29–32. The phrase means "now dismiss" and comes from the first two words of the Latin version of the hymn. The Nunc Dimittis is one of four hymns of Luke's infancy narrative, all of which pick up key Lukan themes. The others are Mary's Magnificat (1:46–55), Zechariah's Benedictus (1:68–79), and the angels' Gloria in Excelsis (2:14). The Nunc Dimittis is spoken by the righteous and devout Simeon, who comes to the temple in Jerusalem, having been informed by the Holy Spirit that he will not die before he sees the Lord's Messiah. The hymn is spoken on the occasion of Joseph and Mary's presentation of the baby Jesus to the Lord. Its main theme is the arrival of God's salvation, which will be "a light for revelation to the Gentiles and glory to [God's] people Israel" (2:32). *See also* Benedictus; Magnificat.

Nuzi Ancient city from the mid-second millennium BC associated with Yorghan Tepe, located on the Tigris River in what is today Iraq. Excavations during the 1920s and '30s uncovered about five thousand tablets. These tablets have been much discussed in regard to the patriarchal history, since some of the social customs have been related to action in Genesis 12–36. *See also* patriarchal history.

O

old earth creationism (OEC) As opposed to young earth creationism, those who advocate the view called old earth creationism believe that the Bible does not speak to the age of the universe, so they turn to science and affirm that the cosmos (and of course the earth) is extremely old. This view is typically tied with the belief that the creation days of Genesis 1 are not literal days, but rather long periods of time. *See also* evolutionary creationism / theistic evolution; intelligent design (ID); young earth creationism (YEC).

onomatopoeia A term that refers to words that imitate a sound. In English, "swoosh" would be an example. In the Bible, the Hebrew of Judges 5:22, which speaks of the hammering of horses' hooves as they gallop, sounds like hooves as they hit the ground: *'Az halemu 'iqqebey-sus madharot daharot 'abbiraw.*

orality While the Bible as we know it is in written form, some scholars believe that what we now have was originally passed down by word of mouth until it was finally written down. This theory is unproven and, if true, may be correct only for certain portions of Scripture. Often the theory of oral origins and transmission also suggests that during this phase the tradition was fluid but that, once written down, it achieved a fixed form. Advocates of the theory that oral transmission precedes written text support their idea by appeal to other literary traditions such as classical Greek and Yugoslavian epic poetry.

oral tradition *See* orality.

Origen (ca. 185–251) Early church father, biblical scholar, theologian, and ascetic. He was perhaps the greatest intellect of the early centuries of the postapostolic church, writing prolifically on topics of textual criticism, exegesis, theology, apologetics, and practical theology. He wrote commentaries on most books of the Bible, interpreting Scripture from both a historical and an allegorical perspective. His most remarkable work was the *Hexapla*, a massive, sixteen-volume work that placed six versions of the Bible in parallel columns. Born and raised in Alexandria, Egypt, Origen later traveled to Arabia, Caesarea, Syria, Greece, and Rome. He was arrested and tortured during the persecutions of the Roman emperor Decius. Though he survived the torture, he died several years later of complications from his injuries. Origen was never canonized as a saint because of later accusations of his unorthodoxy. The Second Council of Constantinople (553) pronounced fifteen anathemas against him related to his teaching on the preexistence of souls, ultimate salvation of all creatures (even Satan), the subordination of the Son to the Father, and other teachings. See also *Hexapla*.

ossuary A stone chest or box used for burial in Israel during the Second Temple period. After death a body would be placed on a shelf in a tomb and allowed to decompose. The bones would then be taken and placed in an ossuary, which was stored on a shelf in the tomb. Often ossuaries contained the bones of several family members. The name of the family and those of the individuals interred inside were often inscribed on the box. Some ossuaries that have been discovered have great significance for the NT. The ossuary of the crucified victim named Yehohanan ben Hagkol confirms that crucifixion victims were sometimes given noble burials. Another ossuary containing the bones of a sixty-year-old man is inscribed with the name "Joseph son of Caiaphas," likely the high priest (whom the NT simply calls Caiaphas) under whom Jesus was crucified. A controversial ossuary with the inscription "James son of Joseph, brother of Jesus" has been the topic of much scholarly debate as to its authenticity.

ostraca Broken pieces of pots on which there is writing. *See also* Arad ostraca; Lachish letters.

Oxyrhynchus papyri A large collection of manuscripts discovered in the late nineteenth and early twentieth centuries at an ancient garbage dump near Oxyrhynchus in Egypt. The discovery includes thousands of Greek and Latin manuscripts of all kinds, dating from the first through sixth centuries AD. In addition to everyday documents, there are many literary works, both secular and religious, including books from the OT and NT and extrabiblical Jewish and Christian literature. Perhaps most interesting are portions of several apocryphal gospels (*Thomas, Mary, Peter, James*), apocryphal "acts" (*of Paul and Thecla, Peter, John*) and fragments from previously unknown gospels (mss. 210, 840, 1224; third–fourth centuries).

P

paleography The scientific study of the age of manuscripts by the analysis of handwriting. Since handwriting styles change over the years, experts can discern the approximate date of a manuscript through the features of its handwriting.

Papias (ca. 70–160) Early church father and bishop of Hierapolis in Asia Minor, an important witness to the authorship and origin of the canonical Gospels. Papias wrote a five-volume work called *Exposition of the Sayings of the Lord*, which is now lost except for citations from the early church father Irenaeus (ca. 180) and the church historian Eusebius (ca. 320). Irenaeus identifies Papias as an associate of Polycarp (ca. 69–155; a mentor to Irenaeus) and one who learned from John the apostle. In his writings Papias provides significant (though disputed) information concerning the authorship and production of the Gospels—information he received from "the Elder John." This John may be the apostle, though he is considered by Eusebius and some others to be a different John. Perhaps most significantly, Papias reports that Mark was Peter's interpreter and recorded his preaching about Jesus. *See also* Eusebius of Caesarea; Irenaeus.

papyrus, papyri Papyrus is writing material made from the pith of the papyrus plant, a reed grown in marshy climates. Our earliest NT manuscripts were written on papyrus. The plural, "papyri," refers to documents made of papyrus. *See also* minuscule; parchment; uncial.

parable A short story meant to teach a particular theological or moral truth. The terms commonly translated "parable" in both Hebrew (*mashal*) and Greek (*parabolē*) have a much wider range of meaning. *Mashal* can mean a parable, proverb, saying, similitude, poem, oracle, taunt, and so on. Similarly, *parabolē* can mean parable, speech, proverb, simile, riddle, illustration, maxim, comparison, and so on. A parable proper is a short story or extended simile that teaches a spiritual truth. There are parables in the OT, such as Nathan's story of a man and his lamb (2 Sam. 12:1–9), told to David after his sin with Bathsheba. The most famous parables in the Bible are those of Jesus, a master storyteller. Jesus's parables of the kingdom, such as the parable of the sower (appearing in all three Synoptic Gospels), define the nature and growth of the kingdom of God—Jesus's central message. Many of Jesus's most well-known parables appear in Luke's central section, known as the travel narrative or journey to Jerusalem (Luke 9:51–19:27). These include the parables of the good Samaritan, of the rich fool, of the great banquet, of the prodigal son, of the shrewd manager, of the rich man and Lazarus, of the persistent widow, and of the Pharisee and the tax collector.

Throughout church history there has been a great deal of misinterpretation of the parables by those who find in them a complex array of allegorical connections. Although parables may contain allegorical elements, they generally make one key point. Adolf Jülicher (1857–1938), in particular, argued that Jesus's parables were not allegories and that allegorical features found in them were the result of later editing by the early church. This, however, would seem to be going beyond the evidence. Although there has certainly been excessive allegorization in the history of the church, many of Jesus's parables do contain allegorical features. There is little doubt, for example, that the parable of the prodigal son allegorizes God's free forgiveness of sinners and tax collectors in Jesus's ministry and the opposition by the religious leaders (represented by the older brother). These allegorical elements fit the historical context of Jesus's ministry. The interpretive key is to place the parables in the context of Jesus's ministry and to relate them to his proclamation of the kingdom of God.

paraenesis "Paraenetic" (adj.) applies to rhetoric intended to provoke the reader to response. "Paraenesis" (n.) is literature focused on practical application and is sometimes contrasted with more strictly doctrinal material. For example, the letter to the Hebrews has doctrinal teaching related to the superiority of Christ and the new covenant interspersed with paraenetic calls to remain faithful in the face of suffering.

parallelism "Parallelism" refers to the relationship between cola (*see* colon, cola) of a poetic line; though not all biblical poetry has parallelism, the vast majority does. There is both semantic and grammatical parallelism. In semantic parallelism, a poetic line echoes the thought of the first colon in subsequent cola (usually there is only one more colon, but sometimes three or more) so that the following cola carry forward the thought of the first by sharpening or intensifying the idea initially presented. James Kugel described parallelism as "A (the first colon), what's more B (the second)." This often works with the use of near synonyms (what used to be called synonymous parallelism), for instance, "Why do the nations rage (A) and the peoples plot in vain? (B)" (Ps. 2:1). Occasionally, parallelism works with antonyms ("Idle hands make one poor (A), but diligent hands bring riches (B)" (Prov. 10:4). To read poetry well, one must ask how the second and following cola further the thought of the first colon. Grammatical parallelism is a pattern of word order and syntax shared by cola within the poetic line. *See also* colon, cola; Kugel, James; poetry.

paraphrase To restate using different words, generally for the purpose of simplification and clarification. While idiomatic Bible translations are sometimes called "paraphrases," from a linguistic perspective a true translation transfers meaning *from one language to another*, while a paraphrase is the simplification of a text *within the same language*. *The Living Bible* (1971) was a true paraphrase since it was produced by simplifying another English version, the American Standard Version. The New Living Translation (1996) is a translation, however, since it is an idiomatic translation from the Hebrew and Greek. See also *Living Bible, The.*

parataxis *See* hypotaxis.

parchment Material made from treated animal skins and used for writing. Many of the early manuscripts of the OT and NT are written on parchment. *See also* minuscule; papyrus, papyri; uncial.

paronomasia A play on words, also called a pun, that exploits the use of two or more meanings of the same word or similar-sounding words for a humorous or rhetorical effect. Isaiah 5:7 represents paronomasia in Hebrew when Isaiah says God "expected justice [*mišpāṭ*] but saw injustice [*miśpāḥ*]; he expected righteousness [*ṣᵉdāqâ*], but heard cries of despair [*ṣᵉʿāk*]." Similarly, when Jesus says of the religious leaders that they "strain out a gnat, but gulp down a camel!" (Matt. 23:24), he is probably exploiting the similar Aramaic words for "gnat" (*qalmâ*) and "camel" (*gamlâ*).

parousia Greek word that could be translated "presence," "coming," or "arrival." It is frequently used in the NT of the return of Christ (Matt. 24:3, 27, 37; 1 Cor. 15:23; 1 Thess. 2:19; 3:13; 4:15; 5:23; James 5:7; 2 Pet. 3:4; 1 John 2:28) and has become a technical term in biblical studies for the second coming.

passion narrative Designation given to the account of Jesus's suffering and death in the four Gospels, including the plot against him, the Last Supper, his arrest, trial, crucifixion, and burial. Form and source critics generally view the passion narrative as the first connected narrative in the oral transmission of the story of Jesus and perhaps the first part of the Jesus story to be put down in written form.

Pastoral Epistles Traditional title given to the NT letters 1 and 2 Timothy and Titus. The title refers to the fact that these letters give guidance for pastoral leadership over churches to two of Paul's disciples. The Pastoral Epistles are the most disputed of the Pauline letters. If written by Paul, they were his last letters known to us, written after his first Roman imprisonment.

patriarchal history The middle section of Genesis (chaps. 12–36) describes the lives of Abraham, Isaac, and Jacob, who are commonly called the patriarchs, or fathers, of the (Jewish) faith. Abraham received the divine promise that his descendants would become a great nation and that God would bless them and through them God would bless the entire world (12:1–3). This promise was passed by Abraham to his son Isaac, who in turn passed it on to his son Jacob. Later Scripture will refer to God as the God of Abraham, Isaac, and Jacob.

Paulinist Term used of someone who follows or reproduces the theological perspective of the apostle Paul. In biblical studies the term has sometimes been used of the writers of books considered to be deutero-Pauline, meaning written pseudonymously in Paul's name by his disciples after his death. The term is sometimes also applied to 1 Peter, since that letter contains many themes recalling Paul's own theology.

Pax Romana Latin for "Roman peace" and referring to the period of Roman domination of the Mediterranean region initiated and consolidated by Caesar Augustus, the first Roman emperor (ruled as emperor from 27 BC to AD 14). During this period of relative tranquility, which is generally dated from 27 BC to the late second or early third century AD, the Mediterranean came to be viewed as a "Roman lake."

Pentateuch Also known as the Torah. Pentateuch means "five scrolls" and refers to the first five books of the OT (Genesis, Exodus, Leviticus, Numbers, and Deuteronomy). While these books are of disputed authorship, it is clear that their final form is a coherent literary whole. The reason why this work is divided into five parts is that a single scroll could not hold the whole composition. *See also* Documentary Hypothesis.

Pentecost Jewish festival that occurred fifty days after Passover. "Pentecost" means "fiftieth day." The festival is also called the Festival of Weeks (Deut. 16:10) and Festival of Harvest (Exod. 23:16). The festival began as a harvest festival but came to commemorate God's covenant with Israel established at Mount Sinai. The festival took on new meaning for the followers of Jesus when—after his ascension to the right hand of God—Jesus poured out the Holy Spirit on his people (Acts 2:1–41). This endowment of the Spirit marked the birth of the church and the beginning of the new age of salvation (Joel 2:28–32).

performance criticism A relatively new methodology that views the Gospels not as literature per se but as a written record of oral performance. Performance criticism starts with the assumptions that the culture of the first-century Greco-Roman world was primarily oral and that the great majority of people saw texts performed, rather than reading them. The Gospels ought, then, to be studied as "remnants" of oral performances rather than polished literary works. Performance criticism is often interdisciplinary, bringing together expertise in such fields as oral culture, speech arts, social identity, collective memory, literacy, classical rhetoric, and so on.

pericope A section of Scripture that forms a coherent unit of thought or a narrative event. The term is most commonly used with reference to the Synoptic Gospels, with their strings of short, semi-independent stories, miracles, and parables.

Persia Cyrus the Great (ca. 580–529 BC) took a relatively small regional power in western Iran and through diplomacy and battle created an empire in the Near East not seen before. His greatest victory, and the one that brought the province of Judah/Yehud into its orbit, was over Babylon in 539 BC. Persia then initiated a foreign policy that allowed Babylon's former vassals, including Judah, to return to their homelands and rebuild their temples. Thus, the postexilic period in Israel began. The events of

Ezra-Nehemiah and Esther take place during the period of Persian rule. The Persian Empire lasted until circa 330 BC, when Alexander the Great defeated Darius III. *See also* Cyrus Cylinder; postexilic period.

personification Presenting inanimate objects or abstract ideas as if they were persons. For instance, the book of Proverbs presents wisdom as a woman in 1:20–33; 8:1–36; 9:1–6. Personification allows the composer to present a concept with greater clarity and vividness. Proverbs speaks directly to young men, and the presentation of wisdom as a woman heightens its appeal and also suggests an intimate relationship.

pesher *See* Dead Sea Scrolls.

Peshitta The traditional Syriac translation of the Bible, probably produced beginning in the second century AD. Syriac is a dialect of western Aramaic. Some scholars have claimed that an Aramaic NT of the Peshitta preceded the Greek and so contains the original Aramaic words of Jesus. The consensus of scholarship, however, is that the OT of the Peshitta was translated from Hebrew and the NT was translated from Greek. *See also* Aram, Aramaic; Syriac.

Pharisees A Jewish sect that flourished in Israel during the Second Temple period. Their chief opponents were the Sadducees. Though their origin is uncertain, the Pharisees likely arose from the Hasidim, the pious Jews who opposed the hellenization of Israel during the period of Seleucid domination and the persecutions of Antiochus IV "Epiphanes." After the Maccabees gained independence from the Seleucids, the Pharisees began to withdraw their support because of opposition to the increasing hellenization of the later Maccabees (the term Pharisee probably means "separatist"). The Pharisees are best known for their strict adherence to the law of Moses, including not only the written law but also the oral "tradition of the elders" (Mark 7:3) that had been passed down for generations. *See also* Hasidim; Maccabees, Maccabean revolt; Sadducees.

Philistia In the twelfth century BC, as part of a widespread dislocation of peoples through the eastern Mediterranean, a group from the Aegean region resettled on the southern coast of Israel and pushed inland, threatening Israel's place in the land. The threat was particularly strong during the period of the judges (see the Samson story in Judg. 13–16) and the time of Saul and David. Important Philistine cities included Gath, Gezer, Ekron, Ashkelon, and Ashdod. The mention of Philistines in the book of Genesis is considered an anachronism by some but may represent an earlier incursion into the land. *See also* Ashdod; Ashkelon; Ekron; Gath.

Philo of Alexandria (ca. 20 BC–AD 50) First-century Jewish philosopher, theologian, and historian. Philo was a Hellenistic Jew heavily influenced by Greek thought. He sought to synthesize Judaism with Greek philosophical traditions. He wrote more than seventy works, including philosophical treatises, commentaries on the Bible, and apologetic defenses of Judaism against pagan opponents. Like later Alexandrian Christianity, Philo interpreted the Scriptures allegorically, finding in them teachings parallel to those of Plato and other Greek philosophers.

phoneme A unit of sound in a particular language system. For example, a "b" in English is a phoneme whose sound can be analyzed as a bilabial voiced stop. It is made by bringing the lips together (bilabial) to produce an explosion of air (a stop), while using the vocal cords to make the sound (voiced). Similarly, a "p" is a bilabial unvoiced stop, since it is formed the same way yet not using the vocal cords. Such phonemes constitute the oral dimension of a spoken language system. Phonetics is the study of these sounds.

Platonism The philosophy of Plato of Athens (ca. 428–348 BC) and of those who followed him and developed the implications of his philosophical framework. Fundamental to Platonism is the belief that true reality consists of the world of ideas (which he called "forms") and that the physical world is merely a shadow of this true reality. These transcendent forms represent eternal and unchanging realities that are independent of the changing things of the world that can be perceived with the senses. Further, these realities represent the true cause of human existence and give it value and meaning. Anything created is an imperfect copy of transcendent forms. The highest of all forms is that of "the Good." Though Platonism is primarily philosophical, a number of religious movements arose around the concepts of Platonic dualism. Gnosticism, for example, eschewed the physical world in favor of the world of true spirit.

poetics The study of poetry and its conventions. *See also* poetry.

poetry In Hebrew, poetry is composed of parallel lines arranged in stanzas rather than prose, which has sentences arranged in paragraphs. Poetry uses compact language (*see* terseness), saying a lot using a few words, and thus increasing ambiguity. In poetry the second colon of a parallel line usually intensifies or sharpens the thought of the first (*see* parallelism). Poetry uses figurative language more extensively than prose (*see* hyperbole; metaphor; metonymy; personification; simile). The poets of Israel also used many other conventions, though less frequently than parallelism and figurative language (*see* acrostic; merism).

postcolonial biblical criticism Type of biblical criticism that interprets the Bible in light of the period of domination of much of the two-thirds world by Western colonial powers. Following the decline of colonial hegemony during the nineteenth and twentieth centuries, biblical scholars began to examine how Western powers had influenced biblical interpretation in these colonies, especially with reference to military and political dominance, assertions of cultural superiority, and racial and ethnic prejudice. Postcolonial interpretation often compares the role and influence of biblical world empires—the Assyrians, Babylonians, Persians, Greeks, and Romans—with that of Western world powers.

postexilic period In 539 BC, Persia under Cyrus (the Great) defeated Babylon and inherited the vast Babylonian Empire to expand the core of its empire (located in western Iran). In this year,

Cyrus issued a decree permitting the Jewish people who had been deported to Babylon to return to Judah and rebuild their temple (2 Chron. 36:22–23; Ezra 1:2–4), thus initiating the postexilic period. The initial returns were led by Sheshbazzar and Zerubbabel.

postmillennialism A theological perspective that sees the thousand-year reign of Christ (Rev. 20:1–7) as the gradual triumph of the church on earth through its establishment of the kingdom of God. The return of Christ is *post*millennial, meaning Jesus will come to claim his kingdom *after* the church establishes the kingdom on earth. *See also* amillennialism; dispensationalism; premillennialism.

preexistence Term used for the belief that the soul exists prior to physical birth; also called premortal existence. The Greek philosopher Plato taught the preexistence of the soul, as did the early church father Origen. This belief was condemned at the Second Council of Constantinople (553). Today, the Church of Jesus Christ of Latter-Day Saints (Mormons) holds to a form of the premortal existence of the soul. All major Christian denominations, including Roman Catholic, Eastern Orthodox, and Protestant denominations, reject this belief.

preexistence of Christ Term used to describe the Son of God's existence as one of the persons of the Triune God prior to his incarnation. The preexistence of Christ has been denied by those who consider him to be merely human or by those who hold to an adoptionist Christology, whereby Jesus became the Son of God at a particular time, whether his resurrection, transfiguration, baptism, or birth. The preexistence of Christ is seen most clearly in passages like John 1:1–2; 17:5; Philippians 2:6–8; Colossians 1:16–17; Hebrews 1:2. It is also implied in the many passages that speak of the sending of the Son by the Father.

premillennialism A theological perspective that interprets the thousand-year reign of Christ described in Revelation 20:1–7 as a literal reign of Christ on earth between the second coming and the establishment of a new heaven and new earth (Rev. 21:1). *See also* amillennialism; dispensationalism; postmillennialism.

primeval history Refers to Genesis 1–11, which covers the time from the creation of the cosmos and humanity to just before the life of Abraham. The two accounts of creation (1:1–2:4a; 2:4b–25) inform the reader that when humans were given the status of image bearers (reflecting God's glory and representing him in his creation), they were morally innocent and living in harmony with God, each other, and creation itself. Genesis 3 recounts Adam and Eve's rebellion when they assert their own moral independence from God. The consequences are devastating, destroying the harmony that existed before the fall. Even so, God continues to pursue reconciliation with his wayward creatures. Three stories, connected by genealogies, follow the account of Adam and Eve's rebellion (Cain and Abel; the flood; the tower of Babel). Each of these stories has the same structure as Genesis 3: they recount a sin concerning which God announces and then executes judgment. Each story, with the exception of the tower of Babel story, also has an indication of God's continuing grace: God gave clothing to Adam and Eve, a mark to preserve Cain from violence, and a warning to Noah and his family to survive the flood. Though lacking a token of grace, the tower of Babel story is nevertheless followed by the call of Abraham (Gen. 12:1–3) as God adopts a new strategy of bringing blessing back to his creatures.

pronouncement story A form or genre of Gospel story categorized by form critics. A pronouncement story is an episode that builds to an authoritative statement or pronouncement by Jesus. For example, the call of Levi and the banquet he holds for Jesus (Mark 2:14–17) result in criticism of Jesus by the religious leaders for socializing with tax collectors and sinners. Jesus responds with an authoritative pronouncement: "It is not those who are well who need a doctor, but those who are sick. I didn't come to call the righteous, but sinners" (Mark 2:17). This "pronouncement" represents the central theme of the passage. *See also* form criticism (*Formgeschichte*).

prooftext A generally pejorative term that refers to a text of Scripture used out of context to seek to prove a theological point.

proselyte A person who has converted to a particular religion, opinion, or political party. The term is used in the NT of converts to Judaism from paganism. Luke reports, for example, that some of the Jews in Jerusalem on the day of Pentecost were proselytes (Acts 2:10), and Nicolaus, one of the seven chosen to help the poor widows in Jerusalem, is identified as a proselyte (Acts 6:5). Although Judaism was not a strongly conversion-oriented religion (but see Matt. 23:15), many pagans found the monotheism and ancient roots of Judaism attractive. Proselytes should be distinguished from "God-fearers" (Acts 13:16, 26). While Gentile God-fearers believed in the one true God of Israel and joined in synagogue worship, they had not converted fully to Judaism by being circumcised (for males) and fully keeping the law of Moses.

protasis *See* conditional sentence.

protevangelium Latin word meaning "first gospel" and the traditional title given to Genesis 3:15, part of the judgment against the serpent after the fall: "I will put enmity between you and the woman, and between your offspring and hers; he will crush your head, and you will strike his heel" (NIV). While for some, this is a statement about the fear and hostility that exist between snakes and humans, for others it is the "first gospel," the earliest prediction of the restoration of fallen creation after the fall. It predicts the ultimate defeat of Satan (the crushing of his head) after the wound he will inflict on the Messiah (the striking of his heel).

provenance Term meaning "place of origin" and commonly used in biblical studies for the place where a biblical document was written. For example, the most commonly named provenance for the Gospel of Mark is Rome. The provenance for Matthew is often suggested to be Antioch in Syria. The term is also commonly used by archaeologists to refer to the place where an artifact was discovered.

Identifying the provenance is important to determine the authenticity of such artifacts and whether they were legitimately recovered.

proverb A brief (usually a bicolon) observation, admonition, or prohibition. Proverbs are true when applied at the right time. They do not guarantee results but inform a person of the best route to a desired conclusion. In the Bible, the largest collection of proverbs is found in the book of Proverbs (particularly chaps. 10–31). *See also* colon, cola.

Psalms of Solomon A Jewish collection written pseudonymously in the name of Solomon and dated to the latter half of the first century BC. The *Psalms* were written by Jewish pietists who opposed certain "sinners" who had illegitimately seized the throne of David and defiled the Jerusalem temple. In response God had sent a foreign conqueror who seized Jerusalem and killed many of its citizens (*Pss. Sol.* 1:6–8; 2:3–8; 8:8–22; 17:7–20). These statements likely refer to the subjugation of Jerusalem by the Roman general Pompey in 63 BC. The "sinners" are the Hasmonean priest-kings, who have usurped David's throne and whose political infighting allowed Pompey to seize the city. The collection has traditionally been ascribed to Pharisaic circles, though others have suggested an Essene origin. The *Psalms* are important as testimony to strong Jewish expectations for a conquering Messiah from the line of David (*Pss. Sol.* 17–18). They contain the first use of "son of David" as a messianic title (*Pss. Sol.* 17:21). *See also* Essenes; Hasmoneans; Pseudepigrapha, the.

Pseudepigrapha, the Large collection of mostly Jewish works written during the Second Temple period. The Pseudepigrapha contains wisdom literature, proverbs, psalms, expansions on OT narratives, apocalyptic literature, testaments (last words) of biblical figures, and other genres. Pseudepigrapha means "written under an assumed name" and refers to the fact that much of this literature is written pseudonymously in the name of OT characters. Though, unlike the Apocrypha, these books are not accepted as canonical by any wing of the church (Roman Catholic, Eastern Orthodox, Protestant), they contain a wealth of important background information for the history, culture, social setting, politics, and religion of the NT period.

pseudonymity, pseudonymous "Pseudonymous" (adj.) refers to something written under a false or assumed name. Pseudonymity (n.) is the practice or result of such writing. A good number of the books of the Pseudepigrapha (Jewish literature written between the OT and NT) are pseudonymous. Many scholars also consider certain NT letters to be pseudonymous, especially the Pastoral Epistles (1 and 2 Timothy, Titus) and 2 Peter, but also perhaps 2 Thessalonians, Ephesians, Colossians, and 1 Peter. There is a significant debate among NT scholars as to whether pseudonymity was an acceptable literary practice in the first-century church. If so, it would have been a way disciples honored their mentors, by writing in their name. No deceit would have been intended, and readers would recognize the noble motives of the author. Others argue that there is no evidence for the acceptance of pseudonymity and that those who were caught writing in another's name were always censured. *See also* Pseudepigrapha, the.

Purim Jewish holiday celebrating the salvation of the Jewish nation through the actions of Esther and her cousin Mordecai, as recorded in the book of Esther. After being chosen to be queen by King Ahasuerus of Persia, Esther works with her cousin Mordecai to thwart the plot of the evil and arrogant Haman, who is seeking to eradicate the Jews. Haman eventually gets his due by being arrested and hanged on the very gallows that he has built for Mordecai. Purim is celebrated on the fourteenth day of Adar, which is usually in March.

qal wahomer / qal vahomer Hebrew phrase referring to a Jewish principle of interpretation utilized by the rabbis. It means "light to heavy" and indicates that what applies in a less important case certainly applies to a more important one. An example from the Mishnah reads: "Jose ben Johanan of Jerusalem used to say, '. . . Talk not much with womankind.' They said this of a man's own wife; how much more of his fellow's wife!" (*m. 'Abot* 1.5). There are examples of this literary device in Jesus's teachings. Matthew 6:30 reads, "If that's how God clothes the grass of the field, which is here today and thrown into the furnace tomorrow, won't he do much more for you—you of little faith?"

Qere *See* Kethib and Qere.

Qingu (Kingu) A demon god that plays a significant role in the Enuma Elish. After Ea kills Tiamat's consort, Apsu, Tiamat takes Qingu as a new consort and battles the hero of the gods, namely Marduk. After defeating Tiamat, Marduk executes Qingu and then mixes his blood with clay in order to create humanity. *See also* Enuma Elish; Marduk; Tiamat.

Qoheleth Hebrew name given the main speaker of the book of Ecclesiastes (see 1:12–12:7). His words spoken in the first person ("I, Qoheleth") are framed by those of a second wise man who is speaking about Qoheleth ("he, Qoheleth"; 1:1–11 and 12:8–14) to his son (12:12). Qoheleth is often translated either "the Preacher" or "the Teacher" but actually means "the one who assembles a group" and may be a way of associating, but not necessarily identifying, this figure with King Solomon, who is said to have "assembled" people at the dedication of the temple (1 Kings 8:1–5).

Q source *See* Synoptic problem.

queer interpretation A form of ideological criticism, growing out of the approach of deconstruction and also feminist interpretation, that approaches the text to disrupt and critique from the perspective of gay interpreters and their sympathizers. Queer interpreters pay particular attention to passages that bear on sexuality. They offer "queer readings" that often dispute traditional interpretations of passages. *See also* deconstruction; feminist interpretation.

quest for the historical Jesus Designation given by Albert Schweitzer to the nineteenth-century "life of Jesus" movement he surveyed in his book *The Quest of the Historical Jesus* (1906). Covering the period from Hermann Reimarus (1694–1768) to William Wrede (1859–1906), Schweitzer concluded that the great majority of these biographers created a Jesus in their own image, turning him into a philanthropic nineteenth-century liberal instead of the wild-eyed apocalyptic prophet that he actually was. *See also* new (second) quest for the historical Jesus; Schweitzer, Albert; third quest for the historical Jesus.

Qumran *See* Dead Sea Scrolls.

R

rabbinic Judaism Movement that has its roots in the reformation of Judaism after the destruction of Jerusalem in AD 70. With the temple destroyed, Judaism increasingly centered on the study of Torah, the law of Moses. Fundamental to rabbinic Judaism is belief that Moses delivered the Torah in two parts, the Written and the Oral Law. The Written Torah is to be found in the five books of Moses, the Pentateuch. The Oral Torah finds its culmination in the Talmud. The beliefs of rabbinic Judaism closely parallel those of the earlier Pharisees, in contrast to the Sadducees, Karaites, and Samaritans, all of whom rejected the oral traditions of the Pharisees. Yet the postdestruction rabbis do not explicitly identify themselves as Pharisees. The beliefs and practices of rabbinic Judaism continue in modern Orthodox Judaism today. *See also* Pharisees; rabbinic literature; Sadducees.

rabbinic literature Following the destruction of the Jerusalem temple in AD 70, Judaism was reconstituted around the study of Torah (the Law). Rabbinic debates on legal matters, some of which go back to the first century and even earlier, were passed down by word of mouth from one generation to the next. These are the "tradition of the elders" (Mark 7:3). Originally oral, the Mishnah (meaning "repetition") was eventually put into writing around AD 200 under the direction of Rabbi Judah the Prince (*Yehuda HaNasi*; ca. 135–217). The Mishnah is divided into six divisions, each of which includes seven to twelve tractates containing rabbinic debates and rulings on a wide range of issues. In the centuries that followed, discussions continued and additions and commentary were added to the Mishnah. These additions are known as the Gemara ("completion") and together with the Mishnah make up the Talmud (meaning "learning"), the full code of Jewish law. There are two editions of the Talmud, the Jerusalem Talmud (fourth–fifth century AD) and the Babylonian Talmud (late fifth century AD). The latter is the standard edition and has greater authority. Other rabbinic literature includes the midrashim (commentary and illustrations on the biblical text) and Targums (Aramaic paraphrases of Scripture). *See also* haggadah; halakah; midrash; rabbinic literature.

rapture From the Latin *raptura*, meaning "seizing" or "catching up." The term is a technical one that refers to the event described in 1 Thessalonians 4:17, where the apostle Paul says Christian believers "will be *caught up* . . . in the clouds to meet the Lord in the air" (emphasis added). There is significant debate, however, concerning the timetable of this event. Pretribulational rapturists believe that the rapture will be a silent event to "catch up" the church to heaven before a seven-year period of tribulation on earth. This tribulation period will be followed by the second coming of Christ to establish his kingdom on earth. Posttribulational rapturists believe the rapture is simultaneous with the second coming. After a period of intense tribulation and persecution for believers, Christ will return to catch up his followers to meet him in the air. He will then descend to earth to establish the kingdom. *See also* premillennialism; tribulation period.

Ras Shamra *See* Ugaritic.

reader-response criticism A school of literary theory that moves away from author-centered or text-centered approaches and finds the locus of meaning in readers or audiences. In reader-response criticism, the meaning of a text is viewed as fluid and indeterminate apart from readers, who create meaning through their reading experience. Background, social context, and other factors influence a reader's perception and so are determinate for meaning. Under this broad category is a wide array of methods and perspectives. Some (conservative) reception-oriented approaches focus on the first readers of the text and seek to discern how it would have been heard in a particular sociocultural context. Other, more radical approaches claim that texts are only brought into existence by reading and therefore have no meaning independent of a reader.

realized eschatology *See* Dodd, Charles Harold.

recension The act of revising a literary work, or a text revised in this way. The term is commonly used in textual criticism where, for example, the Byzantine text type is considered by many to be a recension and conflation of earlier textual traditions. *See also* Byzantine text type.

reception history The study of how particular communities have received, interpreted, edited, translated, retold, and transmitted the biblical text throughout history. It is often contrasted with historical criticism, which studies how the texts came to be through oral traditions, written sources, and redactional activity. Reception history picks up where historical criticism leaves off, examining how these texts were received by their original audiences and by later communities. *See also* historical criticism; history of interpretation.

redaction criticism (*Redaktionsgeschichte*) Methodology that seeks to analyze how the authors of Scripture edited (or "redacted") their sources for theological purposes (their *Tendenz*). NT redaction criticism focuses especially on the Synoptic Gospels and arose as a response to the tendency of form critics to treat the Gospels as strings of disconnected traditions rather than as purposeful theological works. Groundbreaking redaction-critical work in the Gospels was done in the 1960s by Günther Bornkamm (Matthew), Willi Marxsen (Mark), and Hans Conzelmann (Luke). *See also* Bornkamm, Günther; Conzelmann, Hans; form criticism (*Formgeschichte*); historical criticism; *Tendenz*.

Redaktionsgeschichte *See* redaction criticism (*Redaktionsgeschichte*).

refrain A repeated line or section of a poem that often structures the poem. The best-known example is found in Psalm 136, where each verse ends with "His love endures forever" (NIV). The repeated use of the refrain may serve to emphasize the idea expressed. Other examples of refrains may be found in Psalms 24, 42–43, 46, 49, 57, 67, 80, 99, 107, and 136. *See also* poetry.

Religionsgeschichtliche Schule *See* history of religions school (*Religionsgeschichtliche Schule*).

retribution theology The idea that God punishes the ungodly wicked and rewards the godly righteous. In the covenant, rewards for obedience and punishments for disobedience (e.g., Deut. 27–28) follow the giving of the law (Deut. 4–26). The books of Samuel and Kings explain the exile by narrating the multiple sins of God's people. The book of Proverbs often connects wise behavior with good results. However, it is a mistake to think that retribution often works out perfectly in this life. The three friends of Job represent a good example of those who go too far by insisting that all suffering can be explained by a person's sin.

Revised Standard Version (RSV) A revision of the 1885 Revised Version (RV), which itself was the first major revision of the King James Version (KJV). The RSV NT was published in 1948, and the full Bible in 1952. Like its predecessor the RV, the RSV used the critical Greek text derived from the earliest available manuscripts and contemporary methods of textual criticism. Though widely used and accepted in scholarly circles and in mainline denominations, the RSV faced criticism from some conservatives, who considered its readings to be "liberal" and who rejected the use of the Greek critical text over the Textus Receptus (the Greek text underlying the KJV NT). *See also* King James Version (KJV); New Revised Standard Version (NRSV); Textus Receptus.

revolution model In the 1960s and '70s scholars (for instance, George Mendenhall and Norman Gottwald) doubted the accuracy of the book of Joshua's account of Israel's entry and establishment in Canaan. They also doubted the prevailing theory offered in an earlier generation that believed that what came to be known as Israel was the result of a relatively peaceful immigration into the land in the early Iron Age. Taking hints from the Bible (for instance, the story of Rahab) and the Amarna tablets, along with a healthy dose of Marxist sociological theory (in the case of Gottwald), they associated the emergence of Israel with a revolt of the underclasses of Canaan, perhaps inspired by a group of escaped slaves from Egypt. This theory, while popular when it first appeared, has largely been replaced by the internal transformation theory among those scholars who reject the biblical claim of a conquest under Joshua or the minimalist assertion that the conquest story was made up by a much later group that wanted to lay divine claim to the land. *See also* Amarna tablets; Gottwald, Norman K.; immigration model; internal transformation model; Marxist interpretation; minimalism.

rhetorical criticism A type of literary criticism that uses rhetorical categories of the Greco-Roman world to analyze how NT authors sought to instruct or persuade their audiences. The art of rhetoric or persuasion was foundational to the educational system of the classical world, and important works on rhetoric were composed by the Greek philosopher Aristotle and the Roman orator Cicero. Rhetorical critics seek to apply these categories of rhetoric to the NT documents, especially the letters of Paul.

rhyme The intentional placement of similar-sounding words at key places in poems, particularly at the end. An English example is "sticks and *stones* may break my *bones*, but words will never hurt me." While many poetic traditions use rhyme to create sound effects, biblical poetry and ancient Near Eastern poetry do not, the reason being that these are languages that are too easy to rhyme (since masculine [*-im*] and feminine plurals [*-ot*] and feminine singulars [*-ah*] end in the same way as do many verbal forms). *See also* poetry.

ritual Set words and actions spoken and performed in a religious context. Biblical rituals include sacrifices, observance of Sabbath and annual festivals like Passover, and other activities associated with priests and sanctuary. The NT establishes rituals like Communion and baptism that are observed in the church.

Rule of the Community *See* Community Rule (1QS).

S

Sabbatical Year Known in Hebrew as *Shemitah* (release), the Sabbatical Year refers to every seventh year, when Israel was commanded to leave their fields fallow (Lev. 25:1–7) and to forgive debts (Deut. 15:1–11). After seven Sabbatical Years Israel was to celebrate the Year of Jubilee. *See also* Jubilee Year.

Sadducees Political-religious party and movement that arose during the Second Temple period. The precise origin of the Sadducees is unknown, but they likely arose from the leading priestly families of Jerusalem, who had supported the Hasmonean priest-kings after the Maccabean revolt. As part of the aristocratic upper class, the Sadducees were often viewed as out of touch with the common people. Their chief opponents were the Pharisees, who had broken away from the Hasmoneans because of the latter's increasing hellenization. The Sadducees accepted as authoritative only the Pentateuch, the five books of Moses, and rejected the oral traditions of the Pharisees. According to Josephus, they also rejected belief in predestination, the immortality of the soul, and the final resurrection. The Sadducees appear to have had special influence over the priestly aristocracy, the Jerusalem temple, and the Sanhedrin, the Jewish high court. While Jesus clashed with the Pharisees especially during his Galilean ministry, when he came to Jerusalem he faced severe opposition from the priestly leadership and the Sadducees. The destruction of Jerusalem in AD 70 ended Sadducean influence, and in the years that followed, the group disappeared from history.

See also Hasmoneans; Hellenism, Hellenistic; Josephus; Pharisees; Sanhedrin; Second Temple Judaism.

salvation history See *Heilsgeschichte*.

Samaria, Samaritans Samaria can refer to the ancient city that served as the capital of the northern kingdom of Israel in the ninth and eighth centuries BC. As a region, Samaria is the area west of the Jordan River between Judea to the south and Galilee to the north. While Samaritans viewed themselves as the true heirs of Israelite religion, from the perspective of first-century Jews, the Samaritans were a half-breed race, the descendants of colonists who intermarried with the people of the northern kingdom of Israel after the Assyrian conquest. They viewed Samaritan religion as heretical, combining pagan religious traditions and idolatry with Israelite worship (2 Kings 17:24–41). Conflict between the two started early, when attempts by the Samaritans to aid in the rebuilding of the temple were rebuffed by the Jews who had returned from Babylonian exile (Ezra 4). The Samaritans subsequently built their own rival temple on Mount Gerizim (John 4:20). They considered only the first five books of Moses, the Torah, to be authoritative and had their own version, the Samaritan Pentateuch. Hatred between Jews and Samaritans reached its zenith in the second century BC, when the Hasmonean king John Hyrcanus burned the Samaritan temple on Mount Gerizim and forced many Samaritans to convert to Judaism. This is the background to the animosity between Jews and Samaritans we see in the NT (John 4:9; Luke 9:52–55; 10:25–37; 17:16–18). *See also* Hasmoneans; Samaritan Pentateuch.

Samaritan Pentateuch The version of Scripture considered authoritative by the Samaritans. The Samaritan Pentateuch contains only the first five books of Moses, written in the Samaritan alphabet. Samaritans do not recognize as authoritative the other books of the Hebrew canon. Like the Greek Septuagint and the Latin Vulgate, the Samaritan Pentateuch is a helpful resource in OT textual criticism, which seeks to determine the original text of Scripture. While most differences with the Hebrew text are small matters of spelling and grammar, others are more substantive, such as the command given to Moses to build the altar on Mount Gerizim rather than in Jerusalem (the Samaritan Pentateuch has an additional instruction to that effect at Exod. 20:17). *See also* Samaria, Samaritans; Septuagint; Vulgate.

Sanders, Ed Parish (1937–) NT scholar whose important research on Paul and first-century Judaism helped to launch the movement known as the "new perspective on Paul." Among his most influential works are *Paul and Palestinian Judaism* (1977), *Paul, the Law and the Jewish People* (1983), and *Jesus and Judaism* (1985). *See also* new perspective on Paul.

Sanhedrin The Jewish high council and highest judicial and legislative body in Judaism. It was this body that tried and condemned Jesus (Matt. 26:59 // Mark 14:55; Mark 15:1; John 11:47; cf. Acts 4:15; 5:21, 27; 22:30; etc.). While this is the traditional view, there is considerable scholarly debate today concerning the history, makeup, and function of this council in Jesus's day. Was this assembly the supreme judicial and legislative court, the high priests' political council, or simply an ad hoc assembly of Jewish leaders? The Greek term (*synedrion*) can be used of various local councils and assemblies (Mark 13:9), and it is only in the Mishnah (ca. AD 200) that we find details of the Great Sanhedrin as the supreme assembly made up of seventy members plus the high priest as president (cf. Num. 11:16). Yet the great majority of the passages in the Gospels and Acts seem to agree with the Mishnah, identifying the Sanhedrin (*synedrion*) as the supreme Jewish council in Jerusalem—made up of the leading priests, elders, and the teachers of the law. *See also* rabbinic literature.

satrap In the Persian period, the name of a regional leader of a province.

Schweitzer, Albert (1875–1965) French-German Lutheran scholar and man of many talents—physician, professional organist, philosopher, theologian, and biblical scholar. Schweitzer is most famous in biblical studies for his book *The Quest of the Historical Jesus* (1906), which chronicled the late-eighteenth- and early-nineteenth-century rationalistic search for the historical Jesus. His conclusion was that these so-called biographies of Jesus essentially created him in each author's own image, turning Jesus into a modern philanthropist, espousing the nineteenth-century liberal values of the fatherhood of God, the brotherhood of man, and the eternal value of the human soul. Schweitzer claimed, on the contrary, that Jesus must be understood from the perspective of first-century Judaism, as an apocalyptic prophet expecting the soon end of the world. *See also* quest for the historical Jesus.

scribe, scribal The Greek word commonly rendered "scribe" (*grammateus*) originally referred to one who worked with documents, either a secretary/copyist who transposed manuscripts or a government official/clerk (Acts 19:35). Yet in the NT the term is used almost exclusively of Jewish experts in the Mosaic law, who rendered rulings on legal issues. They are called variously "scribes" (*grammateis*), "teachers of the law" (*nomodidaskaloi*), and "lawyers" (*nomikoi*). They are often allied with the Pharisees, no doubt because of their similar interest in faithfulness to the Mosaic law, both its written and oral forms. While being a Pharisee meant affiliation with a political-religious party, being a scribe was a vocation. Many scribes were also Pharisees (see Mark 2:16; Acts 23:9), meaning they were trained as scribes but identified with the beliefs of the Pharisees. The scribal office was not gained through inheritance but through knowledge and giftedness. Potential students would come to a respected teacher and seek entrance into his "school." After a period of examination, students would be accepted or denied. The apostle Paul was trained under Gamaliel (Acts 22:3), one of the leading scribes of Jerusalem. The most famous leaders of scribal schools in the first century were Hillel and Shammai. *See also* Hillel; Pharisees; rabbinic Judaism; Shammai.

scroll Before the advent of the codex, biblical compositions were written on scrolls, rolls of parchment or some other writing material placed on two cylinders. *See also* codex.

Second Temple Judaism The first temple had been built by King Solomon around 960 BC and destroyed by the Babylonians in 587 BC. "The Second Temple period," therefore, refers to the period from the rebuilding of the temple after the Babylonian exile (ca. 516 BC) to its destruction by the Romans in AD 70. Though King Herod the Great massively expanded and remodeled the temple, this temple is still referred to as the Second Temple. "Second Temple period" is therefore roughly synonymous with "intertestamental period," which refers to the time from the completion of the last OT book (Malachi, ca. 433 BC) to the coming of Jesus and the writing of the NT. Scholars more commonly use "Second Temple period," since it is an acceptable designation for both Christians and Jews.

Semitism Linguistic term meaning a lexical or syntactical feature in a language that indicates the influence of a Semitic language (usually Hebrew or Aramaic). For example, Mark's Gospel has a tendency to start sentences with the Greek *kai* ("and"). This is often identified as a Semitism, since Hebrew verbal clauses tend to be parallel, connected with a waw ("and"). *See also* hypotaxis.

sensus plenior Latin term meaning "fuller sense" and referring to a deeper meaning of Scripture intended by God, which goes beyond the author's intended meaning. The Roman Catholic scholar Raymond E. Brown popularized the term in his influential work *The* Sensus Plenior *of Sacred Scripture* (1955). The fuller sense usually becomes evident through the advent of later revelation. For example, the application of Hosea 11:1 to Jesus's family in Matthew 2:15 would be impossible to discern from Hosea alone, apart from Matthew's later interpretation. The concept of *sensus plenior* is controversial since it would appear to open up the biblical text to subjective interpretations unavailable through grammatical and historical analysis. *See also* Brown, Raymond E.

Septuagint The most widely used ancient Greek translation of the Hebrew OT. The name Septuagint means "seventy" (abbreviated LXX, the Roman numeral for 70) and refers to the legend about the translation recorded in the *Letter of Aristeas*. According to the letter, the translation was commissioned by the king of Egypt (likely Ptolemy II) at the prompting of Demetrios, chief librarian of the great library of Alexandria. Ptolemy made a request to the high priest in Jerusalem, who sent seventy-two Jewish scholars (six from each tribe) to Egypt. These seventy-two produced the text in precisely seventy-two days. How much, if any, of the legend is true is unknown, but it is likely that the Hebrew Torah or Pentateuch (Genesis through Deuteronomy) was translated into Greek in Alexandria in the third century BC and that the rest of the Hebrew Bible followed over the next two centuries. The Septuagint was the primary Bible of the early church, and most OT quotes in the NT follow its readings.

Sermon on the Mount Jesus's famous sermon in Matthew 5–7, which serves as the inauguration of his public ministry in Matthew's Gospel. The sermon contains some of the most memorable of Jesus's teaching, including the Beatitudes (5:3–10), his fulfillment rather than abolition of the law (5:17–20), the antitheses ("You have heard that it was said . . . But I say to you . . ."; 5:21–48), commands to love enemies (5:44) and turn the other cheek (5:39), the Lord's Prayer (6:9–13), commands not to judge (7:1–5), teaching on the narrow and wide gates (7:13–14), the parable of the wise and foolish builders (7:24–27), and so on. The sermon has a (shorter) parallel in Luke 6:17–49. It is debated among scholars whether Matthew is recording a single sermon or a sampling of Jesus's teaching.

Servant Songs In the second part of Isaiah (chaps. 40–55), Israel as a nation is repeatedly referred to as Yahweh's "servant" (41:8; 42:19; 44:1–2, 21). Yet in four passages (42:1–4; 49:1–6; 50:4–9; 52:13–53:12), designated "Servant Songs," there are references to an individual servant. This servant is endowed with God's Spirit

(42:1), brings light to the Gentiles (42:6), and gives himself as an atoning sacrifice for his people (53:4–6, 8, 11–12). Christians have historically viewed Jesus as the fulfillment of the Servant (Matt. 8:17; 12:18–21; Luke 22:37; Acts 8:32–33; 13:47; 1 Pet. 2:22, 24). Interpretations by critical scholars range from the nation Israel (or its righteous remnant), to the prophet himself, to a messianic figure. The identification of the individual servant songs was first made by B. Duhm in his commentary on Isaiah, *Das Buch Jesaia* (1892).

settlement period After the conquest under Joshua, God directed the high priest to cast the sacred lots (*see* Urim and Thummim) in order to distribute the land to the various tribes of Israel (Josh. 13–24). At the time of the distribution of the land, much of the land remained under the control of the Canaanites.

Shammai Famous rabbi of the Second Temple period (ca. 50 BC–AD 30) who was strongly influential in the development of the Mishnah, the code of Jewish law. The school of Shammai (meaning the disciples who gathered around him and the body of teaching he promoted) was more conservative in its interpretation of Torah than its chief rival, the liberal school of Hillel. For example, while Hillel said a man could divorce his wife for almost any reason, the stricter Shammai limited the grounds for divorce to adultery (*m. Gittin* 9.10). According to the Talmud, Shammai was elected vice president of the Sanhedrin while Hillel was president. When Hillel died (ca. AD 10), Shammai gained the presidency, and his views came to dominate the Sanhedrin. After the destruction of Jerusalem in AD 70, however, rabbinic Judaism came to favor the teaching of Hillel. *See also* Hillel; rabbinic literature.

Shekinah From a Hebrew verb that means "to dwell," a rabbinic term used to refer to the cloud representing God's glory that filled the tabernacle during the time of Moses (Exod. 40:34–38).

Shema The most important affirmation of faith in Judaism, affirming belief in the one true God. Faithful Jews are taught to recite the confession twice a day, in the morning and evening. *Shema* is Hebrew for "hear," which is the first word of the confession. It consists of three OT passages: Deuteronomy 6:4–9; 11:13–21; and Numbers 15:37–41. The confession begins, "Hear, O Israel: The LORD our God, the LORD is one. Love the LORD your God with all your heart and with all your soul and with all your strength" (Deut. 6:4–5 NIV). In times of suffering and persecution, these were often the last words on a martyr's lips.

Shemoneh Esreh (Eighteen Benedictions) One of the most important prayers in Judaism, the Shemoneh Esreh is the central prayer of the Jewish liturgy. Also known simply as Ha-Tefillah ("the prayer") and Amidah ("standing"—the posture for prayer), it is to be recited three times a day by all faithful Jews. Most scholars consider the prayer to have originated before the time of Christ, making its themes important for NT as well as Jewish studies. *See also* Birkat Haminim.

Sheol This Hebrew term is sometimes left untranslated, but when it is translated it is often rendered "grave" or, rarely, "underworld." As grave or underworld, it is the destiny of all people, godly and ungodly. A more developed understanding of the afterlife, with different fates for the righteous (heaven) and the wicked (hell) awaited the NT. *See also* gehenna; hades.

sherd A broken piece of pottery. Sherds litter archaeological sites both on the surface and in the dirt. Sherds, though partial pottery, do reveal the process of manufacture and perhaps style. Since pottery types change over time (*see* stratigraphy), the study of sherds will often help establish a chronology for a site.

Siloam tunnel inscription In 2 Kings 20:20 (2 Chron. 32:3–4, 30; Isa. 22:11; Sir. 48:17), we learn that in response to a threat from the Assyrian king Sennacherib, King Hezekiah of Judah (727–698 BC) built a water conduit from the Gihon Spring outside the walled city of Jerusalem into the pool of Siloam, a distance of approximately 1,750 feet (533 meters). In 1880 an inscription was discovered in the wall of the tunnel that celebrated its completion (dated to ca. 700 BC). The tunnel was built by two teams of workers, starting from opposite sides and meeting in the middle, where the inscription was found. The inscription thus provides striking confirmation of the biblical account of the building of the tunnel at the time of Hezekiah.

simile A figure of speech that, like metaphor, compares two things that are essentially unlike except in certain key traits. Unlike metaphor, simile uses the adverb "as" or the preposition "like" to make the comparison. Authors use simile in order to throw light on something that is unknown by comparing it to something better known by the reader. In Song of Songs, the woman asks the man: "Place me like a seal over your heart, like a seal on your arm" (8:6 NLT). Here she compares herself to a cylinder seal that marks an object as one's possession; thus she asks her beloved to mark himself as possessed by her and her alone. Such striking comparisons catch readers' attention, as they must think carefully as to how the two objects of comparison are like (and unlike) each other. *See also* metaphor.

Sinai, Mount Also known as Mount Horeb, the mountain on which God made his presence known to Moses and the Israelites and the place where he gave them the law (Exod. 19–24). The location of this mountain is disputed, but it is traditionally associated with Jebel Musa, a mountain approximately seven thousand five hundred feet tall near the southern tip of the Sinai Peninsula.

Sirach A Jewish book of wisdom also known as Ecclesiasticus and the Wisdom of Jesus ben Sira. It was originally written in Hebrew in Jerusalem about 180 BC by the Jewish scribe Shimon ben Yeshua, who was inspired by his father, Yeshua ben Eliezer ben Sirach. The work was translated into Greek with a prologue by the author's grandson in Egypt around 130 BC. Sirach was widely respected as a book of Jewish wisdom. Though not considered part of the Hebrew canon, it was read and studied by Jews and Christians alike. Some copies of the Septuagint include it. It is part of the Roman Catholic

Apocrypha and accepted as canonical by the Eastern Orthodox church. *See also* Apocrypha, the; Septuagint.

Sitz im Leben A German phrase meaning "setting in life" and referring to the life situation in which a biblical passage or book was composed. The term was first introduced with reference to form criticism, where it referred to the context in which particular oral forms arose and developed. Hermann Gunkel used it with reference to the various literary forms of the Hebrew Bible, such as psalms, prophetic oracles, and liturgical formulas. New Testament form critics like Martin Dibelius and Rudolf Bultmann applied the term to the life setting of gospel forms, such as miracles, parables, and pronouncement stories. *See also* Bultmann, Rudolf Karl; form criticism (*Formgeschichte*); Gunkel, Hermann.

social-scientific interpretation Recent approaches that seek to interpret the biblical text based on its anthropological, social, and cultural context. Particularly significant has been research into the social values of the ancient Near East related to such things as purity/defilement, group versus individual mentality, social status, shame and honor, and patron-client relationships. One general tendency among social-scientific exegetes is to emphasize how much social and cultural factors, rather than merely theological ones, lie behind biblical imperatives.

source criticism Historical-critical method that seeks to discern the sources behind the biblical books. In the OT, the greatest focus of source criticism has been on the Pentateuch (the first five books of the OT). The Documentary Hypothesis proposes four sources behind the Pentateuch: the Yahwist source (J), the Elohist source (E), the Deuteronomic source (D), and the Priestly source (P). In the NT, source criticism has focused especially on the Synoptic problem, the question of the sources behind and relationships between the Synoptic Gospels: Matthew, Mark, and Luke. *See also* Documentary Hypothesis; historical criticism; Synoptic problem.

southern kingdom *See* Judah.

speech-act theory A theory of communication developed by John L. Austin and John R. Searle that views language as performative, not just saying things but doing them. Speech acts have a variety of functions, such as requesting, commanding, inviting, warning, promising, greeting, and congratulating. Speech-act theorists distinguish between locutions (what is said), illocutions (what is performed), and perlocutionary intents (what is the expected response). For example, the question (locution) "Is there any salt?" is actually a request (illocution), expecting an action (perlocution). Speech-act theory is important for biblical studies since any act of communication implies intentionality on the part of the speaker or author. If the biblical text contains speech acts, then there is a definable meaning in the text.

stanza, strophe Hebrew poets composed poems by creating parallel lines (*see* parallelism). In a poem, two or more parallel lines, united by subject matter or separated by a refrain, can compose a stanza. Psalm 98 can be divided into three stanzas: verses 1–3 call on Israel to praise God, who rescued them in the past; verses 4–6 call on all the inhabitants of the earth to praise God, who is king in their present; verses 7–9 call on the entire world, animate and inanimate (by way of personification), to praise God, who is the judge coming in the future. *See also* refrain; personification.

stele, stela A block of stone bearing writing and/or pictorial representations. *See also* Merenptah/Merneptah stele.

Stoic, Stoicism Philosophical school of thought founded by Zeno of Citium in Athens in the third century BC. Stoicism viewed reality as essentially pantheistic; all that exists is one, and all is divine. The highest good is to live a virtuous life, which comes through knowledge. The goal of the Stoic is to seek harmony with nature and with divine Reason and to suppress all excess of desire. The Stoic seeks to rise above the fleeting fortunes of wealth and power and of pleasure and pain. Some scholars have seen parallels between Stoicism and Pauline theology as well as conceptual links between

Stoic divine Reason and Johannine Logos Christology. Paul encounters Stoic philosophers in Athens in Acts 17:18.

Strack-Billerbeck Abbreviated title given to the multivolume commentary *Kommentar zum Neuen Testament aus Talmud und Midrasch* by Hermann Leberecht Strack (1848–1922) and Paul Billerbeck (1853–1932). The work draws connections between the NT and rabbinic literature. It is sometimes abbreviated Str-B. The work has never been translated into English, though in 2015 Logos Bible Software announced that they would produce an English translation if enough preorders were received.

stratigraphy A term pertaining to archaeology. Long-term habitation of a location will often result in the formation of a tel (or "tell"; Arabic for ruin), a raised mound, since ancient inhabitants in the ancient Near East, including Israel, tended to build on top of the ruins of previous inhabitants. Thus, an archaeologist digging into a tel from the surface cuts through different occupation layers (called strata [sg.: stratum]), going from the most recent to the most ancient times. These strata will contain pottery sherds and other material remains that will allow the archaeologist to date the various time periods of the location. Such determination of time period is called stratigraphy. *See also* archaeology; sherd; tel/tell.

Strauss, David Friedrich (1808–74) German theologian and biblical scholar, whose work *Das Leben Jesu, kritisch bearbeitet* (1835; English translation: *The Life of Jesus, Critically Examined* [1835]) shocked the scholarly world of his day with its radical view of the Jesus tradition. Strauss claimed that the miracle stories of the Gospels were neither supernatural events nor natural events misperceived by naïve observers—the two common views of his day. Rather, the stories were myths and legends created by the early church to confirm their developing view of Jesus's deity. Strauss's perspective paved the way for Rudolf Bultmann and the form critics of the next century, who saw the church as a creative community freely inventing events about Jesus. Together with the later work of Albert Schweitzer and others, Strauss's book contributed to the demise of the nineteenth-century "life of Jesus" movement. *See also* Bultmann, Rudolf Karl; form criticism (*Formgeschichte*); Schweitzer, Albert.

Streeter, Burnett Hillman (1874–1937) British NT scholar and textual critic, whose influential work *The Four Gospels: A Study of Origins* (1924) ably defended the two- and four-source theories of Gospel origins. The four sources are Mark, Q (the material common to Matthew and Luke), L (Luke's special material), and M (Matthew's special material). Streeter also proposed a Proto-Luke behind the Gospel of Luke. The book was also groundbreaking in proposing the idea of "local texts" in the textual transmission of the NT. Streeter argued for four families of manuscripts: Byzantine, Alexandrian, Western, and Caesarean. *See also* Alexandrian text type; Byzantine text type; source criticism; textual criticism.

strophe *See* stanza, strophe.

structuralism A philosophical approach developed in the early 1900s based on the linguistic theories of Ferdinand de Saussure and the anthropological studies of Claude Lévi-Strauss. It has since been applied to many fields, including sociology, political science, and literary theory. Structuralists claim that human culture must be understood with reference to overarching patterns or structures. As a literary theory, structuralism asserts that literature functions in conventional patterns. Just as there are rules of grammar in language, so there is a "grammar" of literature that determines how narratives operate. All stories have "deep structure," set patterns that operate below the surface structure of diverse plots, settings, and characters. Certain types of plot movements, character types, and kinds of action are common to all stories. By identifying and categorizing these structures, we can objectively analyze stories. Structuralism was applied to biblical studies especially by Daniel Patte in the 1970s and '80s.

Sumer An advanced civilization located in southern Mesopotamia starting at least in the fourth millennium BC. The Sumerians invented writing for the first time in human history sometime in the thirty-first century BC. Sumerian was a cuneiform language where each sign represented a morpheme (carrier of meaning). Economic tablets, myths, legends, royal inscriptions, hymns, laments, and many other types of literature were written in Sumerian during the Sumerians' dominance in southern Mesopotamia, which lasted through most of the third millennium. Other languages (Akkadian, Hittite, Ugaritic) all adapted a cuneiform writing system to their language. During the third millennium, Sumerian city-states, the most famous of which for biblical studies is Ur, were organized into a league of sorts where one of the citys' kings was the dominant figure. The Sumerians were devastated by attacks from the Iranian plateau toward the end of the third millennium, and eventually the Semitic Babylonians rose in their place as the dominant power in southern Mesopotamia. *See also* Akkadian; Babylon; cuneiform; Hittites; Mesopotamia; morpheme; Ugaritic.

Sumerian *See* Sumer.

superscription As used in biblical studies, a superscription is text written above a composition. Superscriptions occur at the beginning of most, but not all, of the psalms. They may ascribe authorship, historical setting, genre, musical arrangement, and liturgical settings.

suzerainty treaty *See* covenant.

Symmachus A translator of the Hebrew Bible into Greek. His translation, produced in the late second century AD, was included in Origen's *Hexapla* (six translations side by side). Only fragments survive today. While the Greek translation of Aquila of Sinope was very literal, Symmachus's was more idiomatic Greek. Jerome used it while translating the Vulgate. Little is known about Symmachus as a person. The church historian Eusebius identified him as an Ebionite (a type of Jewish Christian). Epiphanius claims he was a

Samaritan who had converted to Judaism. Still others identify him with a certain rabbi named Symmachus ben Joseph. All of these are speculative. *See also* Aquila of Sinope; Eusebius of Caesarea; *Hexapla*; Jerome; Septuagint; Theodotion; Vulgate.

synagogue   A Jewish assembly hall used for worship, teaching of the law, the education of children, judicial rulings and punishments, and community gatherings. Wherever ten Jewish males could gather, a synagogue could be established. The term was used both for the building and for the community that gathered there. The synagogue likely arose as an institution during the Babylonian exile, after the temple was destroyed in 587 BC and Jews were scattered. Most large cities would have multiple synagogues. We know of at least eleven in Rome. The earliest record of synagogue sermons comes from the NT: Jesus's synagogue sermon in Luke 4 and Paul's message to the synagogue in Antioch Pisidia in Acts 13. From these and other, later sources, the basic components of a synagogue service can be determined: the recitation of the Shema, various liturgical prayers, readings from the Law and the Prophets, a homily, and a benediction. Psalms may have been chanted or read liturgically, and in Palestine and Syria, an Aramaic Targum would be read after the reading in Hebrew. In the diaspora synagogues, the Law and the Prophets would likely be read in Greek, from the Septuagint or another Greek translation. Synagogues were usually segregated, with men and women worshiping separately. *See also* Shema; Shemoneh Esreh (Eighteen Benedictions).

synchronic   *See* diachronic, synchronic.

syncretism   The mixing or merging of two different things. Religious syncretism is the amalgamation of one religious tradition with another. Inscriptions have shown, for example, that the Judaism of Asia Minor was at times syncretistic, drawing elements from popular superstition and magic.

synecdoche   A literary device where a part of something stands for the whole or the whole for a part. In the sentence, "He's got fast wheels," "wheels" stands for a car. Psalm 44:6 reads, "For I do not trust in my bow, and my sword does not bring me victory." Both "bow" and "sword" are synecdoches, referring to all one's weapons. In Ephesians 6:12, "For our struggle is not against flesh and blood," "flesh and blood" stands for human beings. Synecdoche is a subcategory of metonymy, in which one thing is named for something related to it. In the saying "the pen is mightier than the sword," "the pen" refers to persuasive writing and "the sword" to military action or brute force. *See also* metonymy.

synonymous parallelism *See* parallelism.

Synoptic Gospels Designation given to the first three of the NT Gospels—Matthew, Mark, and Luke—because of their many common stories and sayings of Jesus and verbal parallels. The term "synoptic" means "viewed together." The question of their literary relationship is known as the Synoptic problem. *See also* Synoptic problem.

Synoptic problem The question of the relationship between the Synoptic Gospels: Matthew, Mark, and Luke. Scholars use the historical-critical method known as source criticism to identify the sources behind the Synoptics and their relationship to one another. The most widely accepted view is Markan priority, that Matthew and Luke both use Mark as a source. A majority of scholars also hold to the two-source theory, which supplements Markan priority with another source, "Q," or the "Synoptics Sayings Source." Q stands for *Quelle*, the German word for "source," and includes material common to Matthew and Luke. B. H. Streeter subsequently expanded the two-source theory to propose the four-source theory, which adds two sources, "M" (Matthew's unique material) and "L" (Luke's unique material) in order to account for the rest of the Synoptic tradition. Other, less widely held solutions to the Synoptic problem include (1) the Farrer hypothesis (also known as Farrer-Goulder-Goodacre hypothesis), which holds to Markan priority but eliminates Q, suggesting that Luke used Matthew for the material they share in common; (2) the Griesbach hypothesis (or two-Gospel hypothesis), which holds to Matthean priority, Luke's use of Matthew, and Mark as an abbreviation of both. *See also* historical criticism; source criticism; Synoptic Gospels.

Syriac The ancient language of Syria, a western dialect of Aramaic. Classical Syriac arose as a distinct language in the first century AD. Together with Latin and Greek, it was one of the most important languages for early Christianity. We have many early manuscripts of the NT in Syriac, and many works from the early church are written in Syriac. *See also* Aram, Aramaic; Peshitta.

T

Talmud *See* rabbinic literature.

Tanak Title given to the Hebrew Bible. It is an acronym (TNK) from the first letter of the three parts of the Hebrew canon: Torah (the five books of Moses), Nevi'im (Prophets), and Ketuvim (Writings). The books are the same as those in the Protestant canon but are arranged differently. *See also* Ketuvim; Nevi'im; New Jewish Publication Society (NJPS) translation of the Jewish Bible; Pentateuch.

Tannaim Designation given to the rabbis of the first two centuries AD, whose sayings are recorded in the Mishnah (ca. 200). Tannaim means "repeaters" and refers to those who pass down what they have been taught. The Tannaim were followed by the Amoraim ("speakers" or "interpreters"), the rabbis from 200 to 500, whose debates are recorded in the Gemara (and hence the Talmud). *See also* rabbinic literature.

targum An Aramaic paraphrase, or interpretive translation, of the Hebrew Scriptures. By the first century AD, Aramaic had become the common trade language of the Middle East, and most Jews no longer spoke Hebrew. In a synagogue service, after the reading from the Law and Prophets, a translator would stand up and provide an Aramaic paraphrase. These *targumim* (pl.) were passed down orally and eventually written down. Targum means "interpreter" or "translator." Because the targumim are highly interpretive, they provide insight into the theological reflection of the Hebrew Scripture current at that time. *See also* Aram, Aramaic; rabbinic literature.

Tatian See *Diatessaron*.

Teacher of Righteousness *See* Dead Sea Scrolls.

tel/tell The word "tel" or "tell" comes from an Arabic word meaning "mound" or "ruin" and refers to an archaeological site, an artificial hill resulting from the inhabitants of a town or city building in the same spot for centuries. *See also* archaeology; stratigraphy.

Tendenz From a German word meaning "tendency" and referring to a controlling purpose or point of view that guides or directs a literary work. *See also* redaction criticism (*Redaktionsgeschichte*).

terminus ad quem *See* terminus a quo.

terminus a quo Latin phrase meaning "limit from which," and referring to the earliest point in time for a particular event (often the writing/origin of a literary work). Its counterpoint is "terminus ad quem," Latin for "limit to which" and referring to the latest possible time for an event. For example, someone might say the terminus a quo for the composition of Mark's Gospel is 50, and the terminus ad quem is 69.

terseness Hebrew poetry uses an economy of words to express its thoughts. The tendency toward brevity may be called terseness and is one of the most pervasive features of Hebrew poetry, along with parallelism and an intense use of figurative language. *See also* ellipsis; parallelism; poetry.

Testaments of the Twelve Patriarchs A pseudepigraphic work that builds on the account of the testament (last words) of Jacob/Israel in Genesis 49. The *Testaments* purport to recount the last words of Jacob's twelve sons. There is no doubt that the work has been edited by Christians, but it is debated whether it is a Jewish work that has been touched up by later Christians, or whether it is an original Christian composition that draws upon Jewish traditions.

Each of the twelve *Testaments* begins by summarizing the life of the patriarch, emphasizing his strengths and weaknesses and exhorting the reader to follow the good. Most then contain prophetic visions, including prophecies related to the coming Messiah. *See also* Pseudepigrapha, the.

testimonia A Latin term referring to collections of prooftexts brought together for various purposes in the early church. Because certain OT texts seem to be linked together in more than one passage in the NT, C. H. Dodd and others proposed that the early Christians produced testimonia, collections of related texts for apologetic or catechetical purposes. The discovery of the Dead Sea Scrolls bolstered this view, since several of the scrolls, such as 4QTestimonia (4Q175) and 4QFlorilegium (4Q174), contain strings of texts that function similarly to the theory of testimonia. *See also* Dodd, Charles Harold.

Tetragrammaton God's special covenant name for himself given to his people Israel. The word Tetragrammaton means "four letters" and refers to the Hebrew name of God transliterated in four letters as YHWH and likely pronounced as Yahweh. The name was considered too sacred to be uttered aloud, so Jews reading the OT would replace YHWH with *adonai*, "master" or "sir." *See also* Yahweh.

textual criticism The methodology that seeks to determine the original Hebrew and Greek texts of the books of the Bible (the "autographs"). Textual criticism is necessary because for many centuries manuscripts were copied by hand, and errors inevitably crept into our manuscripts. The primary text of the OT is the Masoretic Text (eleventh century AD), which may be compared to various editions of the Greek OT, the biblical manuscripts from the Dead Sea Scrolls, various versions of the Bible (Latin Vulgate, Syriac Peshitta, etc.), and the Samaritan Pentateuch. NT text critics have available to them a much larger body of evidence, including approximately six thousand Greek manuscripts and various other versions (Latin, Coptic, Syriac, Armenian, Georgian, Ethiopic, etc.). To determine the most likely reading, text critics analyze both internal and external evidence. External evidence relates to the date and genealogy of a manuscript. Internal evidence relates to the likely tendencies of copyists and authors. For example: (1) the harder reading is usually the better reading; (2) the shorter reading is usually better; (3) the original reading is the one that explains the origin of the other. *See also* Alexandrian text type; Byzantine text type; critical text; Dead Sea Scrolls; Erasmus, Desiderius; masorah; Masoretes, Masoretic Text; Peshitta; Samaritan Pentateuch; Textus Receptus; Vulgate.

Textus Receptus The edition of the Greek NT that lies behind the King James Version (1611) and other classic European versions like the German Luther Bible (1534) and the Spanish Reina Valera (1602). The Textus Receptus has its origin in the work of humanist scholar Desiderius Erasmus, who produced the first printed edition of the Greek NT in 1516. This volume, published by Froben of Basel, was a parallel Latin and Greek text. Other editors took up and adapted Erasmus's Greek text, modifying and correcting it in places. The term Textus Receptus (meaning "received text") came from the preface of a 1633 edition published by Bonaventure and Elzevir, which identified the text as the one "now received by all, in which is nothing corrupt." Unfortunately, Erasmus only had available to him about six Greek manuscripts, all of them from the later Byzantine text type. Today text critics have much earlier and more reliable manuscripts, from which the critical text is derived. *See also* critical text; Erasmus, Desiderius; King James Version (KJV).

theios anēr *See* divine man (*theios anēr*).

theistic evolution *See* evolutionary creationism / theistic evolution.

theodicy A work designed to defend the character, authority, and/or integrity of God. Some theodicies deal with the problem of evil, seeking to explain how a good and all-powerful God can allow evil and suffering to continue in the world. Habakkuk is a theodicy, as the prophet questions God about how he can justify using the evil empire of Babylon to judge and discipline God's people Israel.

Theodotion A Hellenistic scholar and translator of the Hebrew Bible into Greek. His translation, produced around AD 150, was included in Origen's *Hexapla* (six translations side by side). Only fragments of the *Hexapla* survive today. It is not clear whether Theodotion was revising the Septuagint or translating from the original Hebrew. His version was widely used in the early church. *See also* Aquila of Sinope; *Hexapla*; Symmachus.

theological interpretation A recent orientation within biblical studies that encourages biblical scholars and the academy to view the books of the Bible not just from a historical, cultural, and literary perspective but as the church's Scripture—a source of faith, practice, and spiritual formation for the people of God. Emphasis is often placed on three *c*'s—canon, creed, and church. The goal of theological interpretation is to bridge the gap between biblical studies and theology, disciplines that grew apart with the rise of historical criticism and the scientific approach to Scripture. *See also* historical criticism.

theophany From the Greek *theophaneia*, meaning "the appearance of a god." In biblical studies it is generally used of God's appearances to his people, such as the appearance to Moses at the burning bush (Exod. 3:3, 6) and to Isaiah at his call to be a prophet (Isa. 6:1–5).

third quest for the historical Jesus A designation given to a diverse array of Jesus research beginning in the 1980s and '90s. It is a "third" quest because it followed the first modern "quest for the historical Jesus" (the nineteenth-century "life of Jesus" movement) and the "new" or "second" quest—the post-Bultmannian resurgence of Jesus studies in the 1950s and '60s. The third quest is characterized especially by attempts to place Jesus within his Jewish context. The expression "third quest" was coined by N. T. Wright. *See also* Bultmann, Rudolf Karl; Käsemann, Ernst; new (second) quest for the historical Jesus; quest for the historical Jesus; Schweitzer, Albert; Wright, Nicholas Thomas.

Tiamat Along with Apsu, a primordial deity who represented the waters. According to Enuma Elish, their commingled waters produced the next generation of the gods, who disturbed the sleep of Tiamat and Apsu. While Apsu planned on killing the boisterous younger gods, he was killed by the god Ea. Tiamat now was angry, and she was a more formidable foe than Apsu. Marduk won the kingship of the gods by defeating her. From her body Marduk created the heavens and the earth. *See also* Apsu; Enuma Elish; Marduk.

Tigris The northernmost of the two rivers that run through Mesopotamia (modern Iraq) from Armenia into the Persian Gulf. It is first mentioned in the Bible as one of the four rivers that flow out of Eden (Gen. 2:14) and mentioned many other times as a prominent river. The Assyrian city of Nineveh is located on the Tigris in northern Mesopotamia. *See also* Euphrates; Mesopotamia.

Tischendorf, Constantin (1815–74) *See* Codex Sinaiticus (א).

Today's English Version (TEV) *See* Good News Translation (GNT).

Today's New International Version (TNIV) A revision of the New International Version (NIV), published in 2005 but subsequently discontinued in 2009. The TNIV project was launched as a result of controversy surrounding gender-inclusive Bible translation. In response to criticism of its decision to introduce a gender-inclusive edition of the NIV in the UK in 1997, the International Bible Society (now Biblica), which holds the copyright on the NIV, decided to freeze the text of the 1984 NIV and to continue its revision process through the TNIV. This decision was subsequently reversed in 2009, and the TNIV was discontinued. The NIV was again revised, resulting in its 2011 edition. *See also* New International Version (NIV).

Torah *See* Pentateuch.

Tosefta Rabbinic traditions from the late second century intended to supplement the Mishnah. Tosefta means "additions" or "supplement." The Tosefta is composed of the same divisions as the Mishnah and has some verbatim material, but it also contains additions and alternative interpretations. *See also* rabbinic literature.

Tov, Emmanuel (1941–) One of the foremost text critics of the OT in the past century. He also was an early advocate for the computerization of the text of the Septuagint as well as the Codex Leningradensis and the Dead Sea Scrolls. In terms of the Dead Sea Scrolls, he helped reorganize efforts to publish the scrolls after a long period of inactivity. *See also* Codex Leningradensis; Dead Sea Scrolls; Masoretes, Masoretic Text; Septuagint; textual criticism.

tradition-historical criticism Examines the historical transmission of literary traditions and charts how the community may have shaped these traditions over time before the traditions were included as part of a fixed biblical text. Tradition-historical criticism utilizes the methods of source and form and redaction criticism. The study of the earlier form of a tradition often goes back to a putative oral tradition. This type of analysis is interested not only in the tradition and its changes but also in the process of its transmission through time. *See also* form criticism (*Formgeschichte*); historical criticism; redaction criticism (*Redaktionsgeschichte*); source criticism.

Transjordan The region to the immediate east of the Jordan River, where today the country of Jordan is located.

transliteration The reproduction of the words of one language using the letters of another. For example, the Greek word ἐκκλησία is *transliterated* into English as *ekklēsia* but *translated* as "church," "assembly," or "congregation." There is occasional transliteration in the Bible. For example, while the Hebrew מָשִׁיחַ (*mashiach*; "anointed one," "messiah") is usually translated as Χριστός (*Christos*; Greek for "Anointed One"), occasionally in John's Gospel it is transliterated as Μεσσίας (*Messias*; John 1:41; 4:25). Similarly, in Mark 14:36 when Jesus speaks to God as his father using the Aramaic word *Abba*, Mark provides both a transliteration (Aramaic written with Greek letters) and a Greek translation: "Abba! Father!" (Αββα ὁ πατήρ; *Abba ho patēr*).

treaty *See* covenant.

tribulation period A period of intense persecution against God's people and severe suffering for the whole world just prior to the second coming of Christ to establish his kingdom. Though many Jewish and Christian texts and traditions speak of increased suffering leading up to God's final judgment, the doctrine of the tribulation is especially prominent in the theological system known as dispensationalism. The tribulation period is generally considered to be seven years long, with the last three and a half years identified as the great tribulation. The judgments of Revelation 6–19 and the actions of the man of lawlessness in 2 Thessalonians 2:1–4 are generally associated with the tribulation period, as is Daniel's seventieth week (Dan. 9:26–27) and the "abomination of desolation" (Matt. 24:15; Mark 13:14). *See also* abomination of desolation; dispensationalism; premillennialism; rapture.

tricolon *See* colon, cola.

Tübingen school *See* Baur, Ferdinand Christian.

two-source theory *See* Synoptic problem.

typology A type is a person, place, or event from the OT that anticipates or foreshadows someone or something in the NT, particularly the coming of Christ. The fulfillment is often referred to as the antitype. An example would be the way Jesus's life and work echoes the events surrounding the exodus and wilderness wanderings, including such things as his baptism (crossing the sea) followed by three temptations over forty days and nights in the wilderness (forty years of temptations in the wilderness), Jesus speaking of the law on a mountain (God giving Moses the law on Mount Sinai), and, most dramatically, Jesus's death on the eve of the Passover, the celebration of the exodus from Egypt.

U

Ugarit *See* Ugaritic.

Ugaritic The modern name of a language discovered during archaeological excavations (beginning in 1929) of Ras Shamra (ancient Ugarit), located on what today is the coast of Syria just north of Latakia. Ugaritic is an alphabetic cuneiform language having thirty letters. It was written without vowels. Ugaritic is a Northwest Semitic language very similar to Hebrew. The native inhabitants of Ugarit were worshipers of the god Baal, so we learn much about Baal religion from these texts. Since Ugaritic is close to Hebrew linguistically, it also helps us better understand many Hebrew words as well as poetic conventions, metaphors, motifs, and more. *See also* cuneiform; Northwest Semitic.

uncial A type of Greek handwriting, also known as majuscule, used between the fourth and eighth centuries. Uncial letters resemble modern Greek capital letters. Our earliest NT Greek manuscripts are written in uncial text. The term "uncials" is also commonly used to refer to the parchment manuscripts of the NT written with this text type, including Codex Sinaiticus, Codex Vaticanus, and Codex Alexandrinus. *See also* Codex Alexandrinus (A); Codex Sinaiticus (א); Codex Vaticanus (B); minuscule.

united monarchy The brief period when, following the very politically fragmented period of the judges, all of Israel was under the rule of a single king. Saul was anointed as the first king of Israel around 1020 BC and was followed by David around 1004 until 965 BC, and then his son Solomon from approximately 965 until 931. Upon Solomon's death, the kingdom was divided into two parts with two different kings. *See also* divided monarchy; judges.

Ur An ancient city that goes back at least to the early fourth millennium BC, and before that a village, located in southern Mesopotamia and often the head of the alliance of Sumerian city-states in that region. Ur is best known in the Bible as the place where Abraham lived for a time before receiving the call to go to Canaan (see Gen. 11:26–12:3). *See also* Mesopotamia; Sumer.

Urim and Thummim The sacred lots given to the high priest in order to inquire of God's will (Exod. 28:29–30). The historical books record a number of times when God speaks to the high priest through the Urim and Thummim, for instance when God informed David that it was his will that David attack the Philistines at the Judean city of Keilah (1 Sam. 23:1–6; the ephod held the Urim and Thummim). The physical shape of the Urim and Thummim, whose name is best understood to mean "light and truth," is never given, but from the verbs associated with its use it appears that they are dice-like objects. The Urim and Thummim are not divinatory devices, prohibited in the OT (Deut. 18:9–13), since the fact that God can choose not to answer when such an inquiry is made (see at the end of Saul's life [1 Sam. 28:6]) preserves his freedom in a way that divination does not.

V

vaticinium ex eventu Latin expression meaning "prophecy from the event," a technical designation meaning that an author has presented something as a predictive prophecy that in fact has already occurred. Perhaps the most notorious claims of a *vaticinium ex eventu* relate to the detailed prophecies in Daniel 8 and 11 concerning the events leading up to the Maccabean revolt. Though purported to be Daniel's prophecies in the sixth century BC, the extraordinarily detailed description of events related to Alexander the Great in the fourth century BC (Dan. 8:5–8) and the actions of Antiochus IV "Epiphanes" against the Jews in the second century BC (Dan. 8:9–12; 11:2–45) have caused many scholars to treat these prophecies as *vaticinia ex eventu*.

vellum *See* parchment.

von Rad, Gerhard (1901–71) Influential German OT scholar in the mid-twentieth century. He was an able practitioner of historical-critical methods, particularly tradition-historical criticism, but also interested in the theological message of the OT. He developed the concept of *Heilsgeschichte* (holy history), which had a murky relationship to real space-and-time events but accentuated the story's theological significance. Indeed, he reawakened interest in the OT in the aftermath of World War II with its tremendous anti-Semitic sentiments. See also *Heilsgeschichte*; historical criticism; tradition-historical criticism.

Vorlage A German word meaning "prototype" or "template." The term is used in biblical studies of a previous edition or version of a text, or a text that was used in some way in the production of another.

Vulgate Latin version of the Bible produced by the church father Jerome in the late fourth century AD. Jerome was commissioned by Pope Damasus I in 382 to revise the Old Latin text. Jerome utilized a variety of texts for his translation, including a copy of Origen's *Hexapla* (which had six versions side by side). He subsequently learned Hebrew from Jewish scholars so that he could translate from the original Hebrew. From 390 to 405 he translated the whole OT from the Hebrew. Although Jerome considered the books of the Apocrypha to be noncanonical, since they were not part of the Hebrew Bible, he nevertheless translated them, and they were included in most copies of the Vulgate. The Vulgate was confirmed as the official Latin Bible at the Council of Trent (1545 and 1563). *See also* Apocrypha, the; *Hexapla*; Jerome.

W

War Scroll   One of the Dead Sea Scrolls, identified by the designation 1QM, whose fuller title is *The War of the Sons of Light against the Sons of Darkness*. The work is an apocalyptic one, describing the final battle between the forces of God (the sons of light)—including the angels and the Qumran community—and the forces of Satan/ Belial (the sons of darkness), identified as the *Kittim* and Israel's traditional enemies (Edom, Moab, Ammon, Amalek, Philistia). The sons of light are ultimately victorious, and all the enemies of God destroyed. Scholars debate whether the work was written during the Maccabean period or the Roman period. *See also* apocalypticism, apocalyptic literature; Dead Sea Scrolls.

wasf   An Arabic term that means "description." In the nineteenth century, European diplomats in the Middle East heard wedding songs that described the bride and groom's beauty by figuratively depicting their beauty from the head down in the most erotic terms. They informed their colleagues in biblical studies about the similarities between these songs and the biblical Song of Songs, and this analogy helped overturn the allegorical interpretation of the Song of Songs in favor of an interpretation that recognized the song as love poetry. The term *wasf* continues to be used of the "descriptive poems" of the Song such as those at 4:1–5:1; 5:10–16; 7:1–11.

Wellhausen, Julius   (1844–1918) German OT scholar who is best known for developing a theory of the composition of the

Pentateuch built on the previous century's research but fine-tuning it in such a way that it finally convinced the majority of biblical scholars. The theory is called the Documentary Hypothesis and continues to exert tremendous influence in biblical studies to the present day. *See also* Documentary Hypothesis; source criticism.

we-sections of Acts   At various points in the book of Acts, the third-person narrative ("he"; "they") suddenly changes to a first-person plural ("we"), indicating that the author is traveling with Paul (16:10–17; 20:5–21; 21:1–18; 27:1–28:16). The "we" sections show that the author joined Paul briefly on his second missionary journey from Troas to Philippi (Acts 16:9–40) and then rejoined him at Philippi as Paul returned from his third missionary journey several years later (Acts 20:1–17). The author stayed with Paul at Caesarea Maritima after Paul's arrest and accompanied him to Rome (Acts 20–28). These we-sections provide circumstantial evidence for the book's authorship by Paul's associate Luke (cf. Philem. 24; Col. 4:14; 2 Tim. 4:11), especially when combined with the strong external evidence. Some scholars have challenged this claim, arguing instead that the we-sections represent a rhetorical device for describing ancient sea voyages. Such a suggestion, however, is not widely accepted, and the simplest solution remains that the author was at times traveling with Paul.

Westcott, Brooke Foss   (1825–1901) Prolific British NT scholar, theologian, Cambridge professor, and bishop of Durham of the Anglican Church. He wrote various commentaries on NT books and other NT topics. He is best known, however, for the critical edition of the Greek NT he edited with F. J. A. Hort, *The New Testament in the Original Greek*, published in 1881. This text, the first Greek NT to be edited using contemporary methods of textual criticism, sparked a revolution in the history of the text and resulted in the dominance of the (Alexandrian) critical text over the (Byzantine) Textus Receptus. The methods developed by Westcott and Hort (WH) remain foundational for textual criticism today. Where WH have been criticized is in elevating our two earliest, Alexandrian uncial manuscripts, Codex Vaticanus (B) and Codex Sinaiticus (ℵ), to the status of a "neutral text." Most text critics today evaluate the text using a combination of internal evidence (the tendencies of scribes and authors) and external evidence (the age and family of the manuscript). *See also* Alexandrian text type; critical text; Textus Receptus.

Westermann, Claus (1909–2000) German OT scholar who exerted a large influence particularly in the study of Genesis and Psalms. He, like his older colleague Gerhard von Rad, used historical-critical methods, particularly form criticism and tradition-historical criticism but was also interested in the theological message of the biblical text. *See also* form criticism (*Formgeschichte*); historical criticism; tradition-historical criticism; von Rad, Gerhard.

Western text *See* Codex Bezae Cantabrigiensis (D).

wilderness wandering After God freed Israel from Egyptian bondage, they entered the wilderness area between Egypt and Canaan known as the Sinai Peninsula. The books of Exodus, Leviticus, and Numbers record their numerous rebellions against God, who saved them, so after their fearful response to the report of spies who went into the promised land (Num. 13–14), God condemned that first generation to die in the wilderness and not enter the land. The book of Numbers narrates the forty years that they spent in the wilderness while the first generation that God judged died off. At the end, the next generation, a generation of hope, was addressed by Moses in his final sermon, which makes up the bulk of the book of Deuteronomy, where he warned them not to rebel as their ancestors had. Only Joshua and Caleb, two faithful spies, were allowed to go into the land from the adult generation that had left Egypt.

Wisdom Christology The identification of Jesus with divine Wisdom, which is personified as God's associate and spokesperson in the OT book of Proverbs and in some Second Temple literature. Wisdom Christology can be seen explicitly in 1 Corinthians 1:24, where Paul says that Jesus is the power of God and "the wisdom of God." Implicit Wisdom Christology is apparent in John's Gospel, especially in Jesus's identification as the divine Logos, who was present with God at creation (John 1:1–2; Gen. 1). In Proverbs 8:27 personified Wisdom says, "I was there when he established the heavens, when he laid out the horizon on the surface of the ocean." Wisdom Christology can also be seen in Matthew's Gospel, where Jesus says, "Wisdom is vindicated by her deeds" (Matt. 11:19; cf. Luke 11:49), and speaks in words that echo personified Wisdom: "Come to me, all of you who are weary and burdened, and I will give you rest. . . . For my yoke is easy and my burden is light" (Matt. 11:28–30; cf. Prov. 8).

Wisdom literature Wisdom in the OT may be described on three levels. First, wisdom helps people live life well—that is, in a way that maximizes success, defined by having healthy relationships and enough resources to not only survive but flourish. Second, wisdom is not only a practical category but an ethical one as well; a wise person is not only well-off but good. But most fundamentally, according to the biblical concept of wisdom, a wise person has a proper relationship with God characterized by the fear of God (Prov. 1:7 and many other places). If one fears God, then one knows they are not the center of the universe, and such knowledge creates humility and an openness to learn from God and others. "Wisdom literature" refers to those biblical books that reflect on the concept of wisdom—especially Proverbs, but also Ecclesiastes and Job, which express the limitations of wisdom.

womanist interpretation The term "womanist" was coined by Alice Walker (1944–) to refer to approaches to culture, art, and literature from the perspective of African and African American women. Walker recognized that feminist approaches did not necessarily include the perspectives of women of color, especially black women. Womanist biblical interpretation often focuses on issues of racism, oppression, sexual exploitation, and patriarchy. *See also* feminist interpretation.

Wrede, William (1859–1906) German Lutheran theologian most famous for his theory related to the messianic secret in Mark's Gospel. Wrede claimed that Jesus's attempt to silence others who intended to proclaim his messianic identity in Mark's narrative was not a historical reality but was part of the author's scheme to cover up Jesus's unmessianic life (*Das Messiasgeheimnis in den Evangelien* [1901]; English translation: *The Messianic Secret* [1971]). This theory did much to promote the view that the Gospels were not historical narratives but rather theologically motivated propaganda. Wrede also wrote an influential work on the apostle Paul (*Paulus* [1904]) in which he called Paul "the second founder" of Christianity and sought to link him to primarily Hellenistic rather than Jewish roots. *See also* messianic secret.

Wright, George Ernest (1909–74) Important American archaeologist and longtime professor at Harvard University in the mid-twentieth century. A student of William Foxwell Albright, he continued his mentor's emphasis of supporting the essential historicity of the biblical historical narratives as essential to their theological meaning. In doing so, he was a part of the post–World War II biblical theology movement. He was also important in the development of the method of dating through pottery stratigraphy. *See also* Albright, William Foxwell; archaeology; biblical theology movement; stratigraphy.

Wright, Nicholas Thomas (1948–) Leading British NT scholar and retired Anglican bishop, now professor of NT and early Christianity at the University of St. Andrews. Wright is perhaps the most well-known NT scholar in the world today, writing prolifically in both popular (as "Tom Wright") and technical (as "N. T. Wright") venues. His magnum opus is his (projected) six-volume work *Christian Origins and the Question of God*. These volumes include (1) *The New Testament and the People of God* (1992), (2) *Jesus and the Victory of God* (1996), (3) *The Resurrection of the Son of God* (2003), (4) *Paul and the Faithfulness of God* (2013), (5) *The Gospels and the Story of God* (projected), and (6) *The Early Christians and the*

Purpose of God (projected). Much of Wright's work revolves around the thesis that first-century Jews viewed themselves as in some sense still living in the exile and that Jesus came to bring about a new exodus deliverance. Wright has also been a leading voice in the "new perspective on Paul." *See also* new perspective on Paul.

X

Xerxes *See* Ahasuerus (Xerxes).

Y

Yahweh In response to Moses's request that God tell him his name at the burning bush, God tells him to say to the Israelites: "YHWH . . . has sent me to you" (Exod. 3:15; authors' translation). The Masoretes, who added vowels to the Hebrew text, did not add the vowels to this divine name, since uttering the divine name was avoided by certain Jews in order never to take God's name in vain (Exod. 20:7). Instead they added the vowels for "lord" (*adonai*), so that the reader would say this rather than the name itself. This practice led to confusion and the practice of pronouncing the divine name Jehovah rather than the form now considered correct, Yahweh. Even today most modern English translations render the divine name as LORD, in small capitals. It is not clear whether God reveals his name for the first time at the burning bush (YHWH does occur as early as Gen. 2:4 and throughout the book of Genesis, though this was the work of an author who was writing after the incident at the burning bush). Rather than revealing his name for the first time, he may simply be explaining its significance as related to the Hebrew verb "to be," as he explains in Exodus 3:14 ("I AM WHO I AM"). *See also* Masoretes, Masoretic Text; Tetragrammaton.

Yahwist *See* Documentary Hypothesis.

Yavneh *See* Jamnia.

young earth creationism (YEC) The view that the Bible teaches that God created the cosmos, the earth, and humanity in the past few thousands of years. While the conclusion of scientific inquiry points to a cosmos more than thirteen billion years old and to humanity emerging over one hundred thousand years ago, YEC advocates argue that the Bible insists that the cosmos and humanity are no more than a few thousand years old. This view is often connected to the idea that the creation took place over a literal six-day period with a seventh day of rest. *See also* evolutionary creationism / theistic evolution; old earth creationism (OEC).

Z

Zealots A term used to describe Jewish political revolutionaries of the first century AD who sought to violently overthrow the Roman authorities and their Jewish sympathizers. Josephus describes a number of such insurgents who appeared during the first century. He traces their roots to a certain Judas the Galilean, who provoked a tax revolt against the Romans in AD 6 (*Jewish Antiquities* 18.1.6 §23). The Romans and Jewish aristocrats considered such rebels to be criminals and thugs, but most common people viewed them as heroic freedom fighters trying to overthrow the oppressors. Barabbas, the prisoner Pilate released in place of Jesus, is identified as a rebel seized for "murder during the rebellion" (Mark 15:7; Matt. 27:16; Luke 23:19; John 18:40; cf. Acts 3:14). The "criminals" crucified with Jesus were likely Barabbas's associates, Zealot-like revolutionaries. One of the Simons among Jesus's disciples (not Peter) is also identified as a "Zealot" (Mark 3:18 par.; Acts 1:13), but it is not clear if this means a Jew zealous for the law (see Acts 21:20; 22:2) or a revolutionary.

Zion, Mount This name has been used for various locations and in various ways: (1) Originally it referred to the southeastern hill of Jerusalem, on which the Jebusite fortress was located. David captured the fortress and named it the City of David (2 Sam. 5:7; 1 Chron. 11:5). (2) After Solomon built the temple just north of this spot, the term came to be used for the Temple Mount, and (3) by spiritual analogy, for the place where God dwells (Ps.

9:11). (4) Often the whole city of Jerusalem or the whole nation of Israel—representing the people of God—is called Mount Zion (especially in poetry; see Isa. 1:8; this use is also throughout the Psalms). (5) Today, a different location, the hill to the southwest of the old city (where the traditional tomb of David is located), is called Mount Zion. This designation may go back to Jesus's day or even earlier.

Zoroastrianism A religion established first in Persia sometime in the mid-first millennium; its prophet was a man named Zarathustra. The religion was strongly dualistic, with a belief in a good god, Ahura Mazda, who was countered by the evil demiurge. It had a developed view of the spiritual realm as well as heaven and earth. Some scholars believe that this religion influenced intertestamental Judaism and eventually Christianity, particularly in the strongly dualistic worldview of apocalyptic literature. *See also* apocalypticism, apocalyptic literature.

An **Essential** Dictionary
for *Study* and *Teaching*

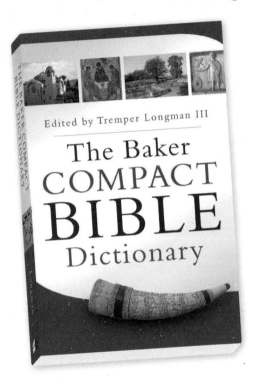

The Baker Compact Bible Dictionary provides access to the essential information and key Scripture references needed to read the Bible with increased understanding. Its A-to-Z entries succinctly define biblical terms, events, people, and places.

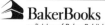